D1367839

Charles Kuralt's **PEOPLE**

Charles Kuralt's
PEOPLE

compiled and edited by Ralph Grizzle

Asheville, North Carolina

Kenilworth Media
28 Kenilworth Road
Asheville, North Carolina 28803

Copyright © 2002 by Kenilworth Media
All rights reserved, including the right of reproduction in whole or
in any part.

Printed in the United States of America

ISBN 0-9679096-1-9

Library of Congress Control Number 2002105780

First Edition

Design by Marjorie Grizzle

Companion web site for this book
http://www.charleskuraltspeople.com

Charles Kuralt's "People" columns were first published in
The Charlotte News. Copyright © 1956 by *The Charlotte News*.
Reprinted by permission of the *Charlotte Observer*.

Also by Ralph Grizzle

Remembering Charles Kuralt
Days Trips From Raleigh-Durham

He was concerned with people. He liked to talk about the lives that other people lived, and he liked to put himself in their places. We'd pick pictures out of the newspapers, and we'd psychoanalyze those pictures: 'Well, what's this person like? What do you think his business is? What type of character does he have?' He studied people.

—Landon Smith, childhood friend, speaking of Charles Kuralt at age 13.

Contents

———

CONTENTS

June

CONTENTS

July

CONTENTS

October

CONTENTS

November

CONTENTS

Preface

———

I was twenty-one years old, a year out of the University of North Carolina, and prowling the streets for The Charlotte News. *I wrote a daily column called 'People.' (That was a more original title in 1956 than it is today.) Each day I would seek out some cop or kid or cab driver and tell his story in a few hundred words. I carried a battered Rolleicord camera over my shoulder for taking a picture to go with my column. I felt there was some kind of romance in my job: I was Damon Runyon, recording life in the streets, except that the streets I had to work were Trade and Tryon rather than Broadway. It didn't matter. I used to walk bravely up to panhandlers and back-alley crapshooters—the sort of people others avoided— and strike up a conversation.*

—Charles Kuralt (from the Foreword to "Suitcases" by Anne Hall Whitt. Kuralt interviewed Whitt's father. His story appears on page 177.)

PREFACE

A S A REPORTER FOR *THE CHARLOTTE NEWS*, Charles Kuralt wrote 170 "People" columns. I stumbled upon them while researching my book "Remembering Charles Kuralt" and thought then that they deserved a better home than the dark, closed drawers where they were stored on microfilm.

It is no small testament to the literary merits of Kuralt's columns that in 1957 they garnered the Scripps-Howard Ernie Pyle Award. The award, then as it does now, recognizes newspaper writing most nearly exemplifying the style and craftsmanship of the great World War II reporter and human interest columnist Ernie Pyle.

While the Pyle award suggests that Kuralt's columns should be stitched between the covers of a book that may be pulled from the shelf and read without having to roll through coils of microfilm, there is a more compelling reason to present these stories in a place where they might live on in the public eye: Kuralt taught us to how to see people. By penetrating the exterior, he found not only meaning and worth in the lives of others but also an interior sheen that was often hidden beneath a dull surface. To Kuralt, all people possessed dignity. His gift was that he looked deeply enough to see it.

Moreover, "People" represents the beginning of a comforting, reassuring and, for me at least, a still-longed-for dialog that Kuralt continued with Americans for more than four decades. Through him, we learned that the world was not falling apart around us, despite the news and images of chaos that the media fed us. Kuralt told us in 1956, and up until his death in 1997, that we were better than we thought we were, more noble than we had imagined we could be and that there was, and is, much to marvel at in our fellow countrymen.

Throughout his life, Kuralt trumpeted these same themes again and again. That's why "People" will ring familiar to anyone who in later years turned to CBS to watch "On the Road" or "Sunday Morning." The tone, style and reportorial substance laid down by 22-year-old Kuralt—trim, bright-eyed and as fresh as the starched white shirt he wore—differed little from that of the balding, roll-bellied reporter who collected 13 Emmys and other awards for his stories of hope and unheralded heroes.

There is startling continuity between the early "People" columns and the work Kuralt did at CBS for nearly four decades. He was, by and large, unchanging. All his life, he found meaning in places where no one else thought to look. At the tip of his reporter's pen, small characters loomed large; seemingly insignificant events symbolized larger, universal truths: One man's desire to grow an orange tree in Charlotte, for example, represented similar dreams tucked away in the aspirations of all.

Kuralt's "People" columns are insightful and poetic—as edifying as they are entertaining and with a purity of spirit that is too good to be buried in microfilm stored and forgotten in dark filing cabinets.

After getting the green light from *Charlotte News'* Managing Editor Tom Fesperman, Kuralt wrote his first "People" column in April 1956, nearly a year after he joined the "largest evening newspaper in the two Carolinas." He penned the daily column for nine months and offered no explanation as to why he stopped writing it at the end of 1956. Even so, Kuralt remained with the *News* several months into the new year, writing front page stories and feature articles before CBS Radio took note of his talents and recruited him to New York in the spring of 1957.

Of the 170 "People" columns he wrote, one, dated December 18, 1956, has vanished. That entire issue of the *News* missed being archived on microfilm. Perhaps someone fortunate enough to find yellowed copies of the *News* stored in an old attic will turn up the missing story one day.

"People" did not appear in the latter half of August. Nor

did Kuralt's byline appear in the *News* during that time. My guess is that the young reporter took some time off from work in the final dog days of summer. September opens with a story filed from breezy Wrightsville Beach, North Carolina, where Kuralt writes about a boy who built a castle in the sand only to watch the ocean tear it down. Kuralt saw elements of heroism in such trivial events. After all, the boy would go on to build other sand castles, despite their impermanence.

Some years before his death, Kuralt was asked why he referred to those he interviewed, whether he found them on the Atlantic shores, the streets in Charlotte or the backroads of America, as "heroes," despite their relative obscurity in a fame-obsessed world. Kuralt responded thoughtfully, "They keep the spirit of the country alive."

I suggest you read "People" in chronological order. By doing so, you will meet familiar faces as you notch off another week or month. Those faces have been absent from the streets of Trade and Tryon for nearly five decades now, tucked away in the dark bottom drawers among boxes of microfilm—an inappropriate resting place for heroes and the young reporter who spent a lifetime telling us stories—about people.

Ralph Grizzle, September 2002

A NOTE ABOUT THE PHOTOGRAPHS:
Unfortunately, the photographs that ran with Charles Kuralt's "People" columns were destroyed. Where possible, however, I have included photographs that I obtained from microfilm archives. As might be expected, the print quality is poor, but given the choice between a poor photograph or no photograph, I opted for the former. If nothing else, the grainy, black and white photographs suffuse the stories with a sense of the time—1956.

Kuralt snapped many of the photos that accompanied his columns. Charlotte News *Photographer Tommy Franklin and his team snapped others.*

April 1956

He did not do a lot of hard-news reporting when he was at The Charlotte News. *His specialty was always the little people.*

—Tom Fesperman, managing editor, *Charlotte News*, who assigned Kuralt the column "People"

Mrs. Goodrum Lovingly Tends Garden Few People Ever See

April 15, 1956

Pᴿᴼᴳᴿᴱˢˢ" ɪs ᴀ ʙɪɢ ᴡᴏʀᴅ ɪɴ ᴛʜᴇ ᴠᴏᴄᴀʙᴜʟᴀʀʏ ᴏғ ᴏᴜʀ ᴛᴏᴡɴ. When somebody decides there is going to be a little progress, a block of old houses is cleared away in a flash and a shiny new building of glass and steel goes up. It's as simple as that.

Only not quite, not always.

Not for Mrs. J.H. Goodrum who, where they are going to build that five-story governmental center on East Fourth Street, is going to lose her flower garden.

Mrs. Goodrum lives with her husband at 710 E. 4th. She is a polio victim who is confined to a wheelchair, so she doesn't work in the ground herself. But every spring, she wheels out to the tiny back yard and directs her mother and Hubert Foard, a young Second Ward High School student, in planting the flowers.

1

And every spring, from the black, cinder-covered earth behind the County Garage, rises a dazzling assortment of blooms—zinnias, pansies, violets, tulips, hollyhocks, Sweet William, Chrysanthemums, periwinkle, roses and lilies.

Nobody sees the flowers but Mrs. Goodrum and her next-door neighbor, Mrs. Hazel Howe, who raises some of her own, and the employees of the garage and an occasional stranger who wanders through the alley.

But anyone who has ever seen it knows it is one of the city's most beautiful—every spring.

Now, though, things have changed. Mrs. Goodrum's father, who also loved the flowers, has died. Her mother is too arthritic to work in the garden. In any case, it looks like this would be the garden's last spring.

Mrs. Goodrum and her husband will have to move, of course, if the government building is built. They can take the two pet dogs and the parakeet and the television set. The roomers who live upstairs can find other quarters.

When progress comes, people have to make way for it, even if that means giving up rich earth that was wrestled from the cinders and made to lend color to a drab alley.

Mrs. Goodrum, after all, has read the newspapers. And the newspapers have carried front-page drawings of the building that is to rise higher on the spot than the hollyhocks ever could.

Worth Heath: Unfortunately, Is Not A Rock 'N' Roll Fan

April 17, 1956

IT IS EVERY MAN TO HIS OWN TASTES IN THIS BROAD, free land, and if your tastes lie in the direction of Rock-and-Roll music, well, that's all right with Worth Heath.

But he isn't having any, thanks.

"I didn't mind it at first," Mr. Heath declares. "But after you've heard Little Richard play 'Slipping and Sliding' a couple hundred times, that's enough."

Mr. Heath hates to think about it, but he's partly responsible for the success of Rock-and-Roll—at least at the restaurants and drive-ins along Highway 49 between here and Randleman. He's the man who keeps their juke boxes full of stuff.

"Two years ago, they wouldn't have it," he says, with the weariness of a man who knows when he's licked. "They had a little Hank Williams, a little Ernest Tubb, maybe a little Eddie Arnold and they were happy. Nice, quiet hillbilly singing. I thought I got tired of THAT—but I'd sure like to get back to it now."

Mr. Heath buys machines at Brady Distributing Co. here and rents out 65 of them to restaurant owners. He decides what goes in them, and, since the public must feel it is getting its nickel's worth, what goes in them is Rock-and-Roll.

The hottest thing spinning right now is Carl Perkins' record of "Blue Suede Shoes," Mr. Heath says.

"If I hear it one more time, I'll be ready for a white leather coat."

Rock-and-Roll replaced guitar strumming and banjo picking next to the public's heart soon after the death of hillbilly hero Hank Williams, Mr. Heath remembers.

Hillbillies haven't had a chance since.

"On six of my juke boxes, I've got classical records," he says. "The real things, Chopin. And you know what's right next to 'em on the selection board? 'Long Tall Sally' and 'Heartbreak Hotel.' "

Mr. Heath wearied unto death of rocking, rolling, slipping and sliding, is biding his time, waiting for the return of mountain music.

In the meantime, there is one customer who helps him keep his sanity—a lady restaurant owner who's got the formula for fighting off the crashing drums and staccato saxes and has used it with formidable endurance.

Worth Heath is grateful to here. She has kept Bing Crosby's "White Christmas" on her juke box for four years.

Martha Farmer Buys A New Dress Especially For Wednesday Night

April 18, 1956

M ARTHA FARMER WAITED 35 YEARS TO FALL IN LOVE. She was beginning to think it would never happen.

Then, last week in the Charlotte bus station, love touched her on the arm and offered her a chocolate milkshake.

It was midnight and Martha, a secretary in Hampton, Va., was on her way home from Greenville, S.C., where she had visited an invalid brother. The Charlotte stopover was a short one. She was tired and hurried and the hot chocolate she had ordered was too hot to drink.

He was standing next to her with a milkshake in his hand.

"He smiled at me," she said. "I can't forget the way he looked—and then, when I told him my bus was leaving, he let me drink almost all of his milkshake.

"He asked me where I was going and when I told him, he said 'I wish I were going somewhere. I live right here ... ' "

That's all they had time for. Martha ran to catch her bus.

When she got home, she mailed a want ad to *The Charlotte News* asking him to call. The *News* carried a small story about the bus station romance. On the third day, the telephone rang. It was he.

"It was wonderful," Martha Farmer said. "We talked for 10 to 15 minutes, maybe longer. He was very nice to talk to.

"I know this sounds funny," she said, "but I've never been in love before. He's coming up Wednesday night ... "

This is Wednesday night. And Martha Farmer, who waited 35 years to fall in love, went out and bought a new dress today.

Thomas J. Hunter
Seeks A Black Sheep

April 19, 1956

DIFFERENT PEOPLE WANT DIF-
FERENT THINGS. Some yearn for
love, some want sports cars,
some want 16-room houses.

Thomas J. Hunter wants a
black sheep.

He's a farmer, 43 years old,
who lives on Hunter Road. All
his life, for no reason that he
can think of, he has wanted a
black sheep.

He called the newsroom
the other day. "Excuse me,"
he said, "but there's a picture
on page A-6 today that I was
wondering about."

It was a picture of a wobbly-legged lamb on an Iowa farm.
A black lamb.

"Could you tell me," he asked, "where that picture came
from?"

It turned out that the picture, an Associated Press wire-photo, had been taken on the farm of Russell Frandson near Story City, Iowa.

"I know it sounds silly," Mr. Hunter said, "but I wanted to write to the man and see if he wouldn't crate up that lamb and send it to me.

As far as Mr. Hunter knows, there isn't a black sheep left in North Carolina.

"I've looked everywhere," he said. "I've been to the Bland place down near Pineville, I've been to see Mr. Gibbons and Gene Cochran and Caldwell Bradford from Davidson.

"They don't know about any black sheep. I went to Asheboro one time to look over a big sheep farm there, but they didn't have any either."

It was an implausible, but solid, impasse.

"I've got 10 sheep of my own, now," Mr. Hunter said, "but no black ones. I want a black one

"Once, Mr. John Pharr, who lived up on Highway 28 near the County Home, had some black ones. He promised me the first black lamb ... but in his lifetime, he never had one born.

"I've been looking for a long time now."

So when he came to town to do some shopping, bought a first edition of the *Charlotte News* and saw a black sheep looking at him from Page 6-A, Mr. Hunter got excited.

Sports cars and 16-room houses are becoming fairly common nowadays. Thomas J. Hunter isn't interested. His dream is rarer and of longer standing.

That's why he sat down this week to write a letter to a fellow farmer, Russell Frandson of Story City, Iowa.

Dorothy Masterson's Plaid Coat Is Part Of Show Business Ritual

April 20, 1956

D OROTHY MASTERSON'S TATTERED PLAID COAT IS PART OF THE VOODOO RITUAL OF SHOW BUSINESS. There's no other way to explain why the fantastic gladrag has followed her around, in cars, trains, airplanes and steamships, in dozens of cities, for performances of more than 200 plays, for more than 20 years.

Mrs. Masterson is director of the Mint Museum Drama Guild and of the Masterson Theater School and a former treader of the boards from Broadway to Colorado Springs.

She bought the coat, a calf-length, strap-in-the-back model, to brighten up the dark days in 1935. That was in Kansas City. She walked out of the store and back to her hotel and found a telegram offering her a director's job at the Memphis, Tenn., Little Theater.

Well, that was that.

"Since that day," Mrs. Masterson says, "I have never directed, produced or appeared in a play without that coat."

It went with her to Memphis, to Decatur, Ill., to New York, to other places along the line. Sometimes a cast member wore it, sometimes it was just tossed casually on the set, sometimes it had to hang backstage. When the superstitious actress was doing radio broadcasts with Victor Mature, it reclined beside the microphone.

And tomorrow night, when Dorothy Masterson's Drama Guild actors read "Don Juan In Hell," at the Mint Museum, the old coat will be nearby, emitting its strange good luck charm.

It will there—or Dorothy Masterson won't.

Arthur House Works In The City, But He's A Farmer At Heart

April 23, 1956

ARTHUR HOUSE, who spends his working hours in the center of the city, is a farmer at heart. He is concerned with pigeons, grass and azalea bushes, and he gets "a good deal of pleasure out of it."

He has always loved to dig in the dirt, to mow lawns and the like. Back in 1948, he heard they needed a yard man at the First Presbyterian Church. He was a janitor at the Builders Building at the time, and perfectly satisfied, but he thought about those three and a half acres of grass and trees, and after a while he went over and took the job.

Now, with the help of James Neal and Sterling Jones, he keeps things neat in the yard, the flower beds weeded, the walks swept clean.

He knows his yard, just as other city workers know their offices or plants.

"That west corner down there, where the grass doesn't grow any more ... It got that way," he says, "because of the children. When the day nursery kids starting coming, it soon got trampled down.

"All that running around is not good for the grass, but it's good for the kids."

When he gets time, Arthur House plays with "the kids" as they're always begging him to—pulls them on their roller skates or throws a softball to them.

But he has a lot of other things to keep him busy. He has to keep pigeons out of the dark, inviting church sanctuary, feed a three-legged squirrel who has difficulty foraging for his own food, and keep the bird-bath full.

All the little things, like the leaves he rakes in the fall and the blades of grass he tends in the spring, rural things that he enjoys all the more because he is ringed in by tall buildings and city streets while doing them.

"You have to work hard," he said, "but it's better than being a janitor somewhere where you don't see the trees or anything. People really enjoy walking through here. There's one lady who comes every afternoon to feed the squirrels ... "

He stood with his arms crossed and looked over the yard, down to the west corner where there isn't any grass and over to the Church St. side where the tallest elms grow.

He said, "I hope they never change it—build a building here or anything.

"I don't know what I'd do."

Rev. Shelton M. Hutchison Considers Ways Of The Ant

April 24, 1956

H E PLAYS MUSICAL INSTRUMENTS, for one thing—which is not so unusual except he plays 20 of them, including such unlikely ones as bagpipes, xylophone and glockenspiel.

He collects fossils. He collects minerals. He also collects coins, buttons, antiques, music boxes and coats of arms.

He operates an entertainers' bureau.

He runs his own real estate agency.

He reads Hebrew and Greek.

He fishes and plays golf.

He debates and lectures and preaches.

The Rev. Shelton M. Hutchison does none of these things in a half-hearted way. When he goes about playing the bagpipes, he does it with full lungs and a hefty tone. When he starts to collect coins, nothing will do but that he collect a British penny for every year they have been minted. When he reads Greek, he reads with the intonations of a Homer.

The McGee Presbyterian Church's former minister has done some traveling in his time—to Europe twice (and he's going again next month) and to 44 American states. Now he has come home to the fine old house at 3939 Providence Rd., where six generations of Hutchisons have lived before him.

He has changed the house a little, though. Being Shelton M. Hutchison, he had to.

He has built his own heating system—from cast-off refrigerator coils. Slabs of marble picked up over the years now form a dazzling walkway through the yard. And behind the house (where he built the first public golf course in North Carolina years ago) is one of Mecklenburg's most appealing real estate developments. It still bears the name of the golf course—Mammoth Oaks—but putting greens have been transformed into lawns and the water hazards have become frontyard fishponds.

Mr. Hutchison belongs to dozens of organizations and is active in almost all of them—especially the 108th Division, Army Reserve, which he serves as chaplain.

His neighbors declare he's a genius, but, they add, he has help. Mrs. Hutchison, the 1928 "Miss Kentucky," is a charming, talented lady who matches her husband enthusiasm for enthusiasm.

In one of Shelton Hutchison's score of Bibles is checked a passage from Proverbs: "Go to the ant, thou slaggard; consider her ways and be wise."

So the Rev. Mr. Hutchison, who must keep that admonition tucked away permanently in his astonishing mind, proceeds to brush up on his lecture, "Fifty-Seven Things You've Never Seen 'Til Now" . . .

Or to re-read one of his 2,000 books ...

Or to turn out a few hundred yardsticks on his home-made machinery out in the barn ...

How A Conductor Left Charlotte After Trying To Build Symphony

April 25, 1956

A DISAPPOINTED YOUNG MAN LEFT CHARLOTTE IN 1919 after concluding there just wasn't any interest in getting a symphony orchestra started here.

He had tried, and despite the encouragement of David Ovens—then, as now, the spearhead of musical Charlotte—he had failed.

He left town a little regretfully, because it was in Charlotte that he had gotten his start as a symphonic conductor.

Mr. Ovens had noticed his way with the choral group at Charlotte's sprawling Army installation, Camp Greene, where the young man had been music director.

"I remember thinking he had tremendous ability," Mr. Ovens says. "I thought he was just the man to direct the chorus at our 'Spring Festival.' "

This was a big chance for an unsung musician—a chance to conduct the Metropolitan Opera orchestra, which accompanied the chorus, and to receive his first newspaper reviews.

When the festival was over, the young conductor had an idea—why not form a permanent "Symphony of the

Carolinas" with headquarters in Charlotte? He labored at it for a while. But he couldn't whip up the necessary interest. The idea failed.

The young conductor said goodbye to his friends in Charlotte and turned north to New York.

But the dream he had, the dream of an orchestra that would play great music for the community, stayed alive. A dozen years later, some of his Charlotte friends finally founded the Charlotte Symphony.

And this week, as the Symphony began its 25th Anniversary fund drive, those friends got a letter from the conductor.

He called the Charlotte Symphony "my dream child of 1919" and extended "my congratulations and best wishes upon reaching your 25th Anniversary."

The writer was no longer young, and no longer unsung. He is conductor now of the world-famous Firestone Orchestra and few lovers of music have not heard the name he signed to his letter.

"Very Sincerely

"Howard Barlow."

Ernest Friday Has Witnessed Changes In Tonsorial Habits

April 26, 1956

O NE DAY IN 1903, the shopboy at the old Benbow Hotel barber shop in Greensboro gestured to a newspaperboy on the street and asked him, "How'd you like to have a free haircut?"

The newspaperboy was doubtful, but agreeable, and Ernest Friday's barbering career was underway.

Now, you can sit in Charlotte's oldest barber shop, Thad L. Tate's on E. 4th St., and hear about that career.

A brass cuspidor rests in the middle of the floor and a ceiling fan revolves lazily in the spring and summer. Mr. Friday's talk blends right into the noise of the fan, the snip of scissors, the buzz of electric clippers:

"I've cut men's hair on the board, when they were children, and now I'm cutting their children's hair on the board ... You take Mr. Edwards, the broker. He's been coming to the shop since 1889, and so has Mr. Jim Bell, the father of Spencer Bell, and there may be some others.

"I worked in Greensboro and had my own shop in Mooresville and worked for Mr. Tate until he died, and I have learned a few things.

"For example, if a customer comes in and doesn't start a conversation, I won't. I tell him I hope he's feeling good and ask him what he wants. If it's a shave, I asked him whether he wants it one over or close. Some barbers to my mind talk too much. I've told them so, but it doesn't do any good.

"A man—a new customer—once told Mr. Tate, 'I came in here for a haircut and not for a social visit. I want you to give me a haircut and let me go.'

"Well, Mr. Tate waited on him 40 years and never had another word with him until the man got wealthy and softened a bit. Then he didn't mind talking because he didn't have anything to worry about."

In the course of cutting your hair, Mr. Friday will tell you the years have bought changes to the business:

"There was a time when if a man wasn't a good shaver, he wasn't a good barber. Ninety percent of all the customers shaved in the barber shop. Now, when a man gets a shave, it's because he's in a hurry.

"Nowadays, customers want you to work fast and let them go. A few years ago, if you rushed a man, he might quit you and not give you any reason.

"In the Camp Greene days, around 1917 and 1918, we had a barber who gave a man a haircut, shampoo, shave and tonic in 12 minutes—rushing to get to the soldier officers.

"But it's never been a custom of mine to rush one man to get to another. My stepfather told me when I first started, 'Do everything you can to please that old customer and send him off feeling happy,' and that's the way I've always done it."

Louis Kraar Didn't Understand Why The Spotlight Rested On Him

April 27, 1956

LOUIS KRAAR, standing there with the spotlight in this eyes and the waves of applause in his ears, just couldn't understand it.

The Charlotte senior at the University of North Carolina had never been a very popular student. He had chosen another role on purpose.

Four years ago, his first day on the campus, he had walked into the *Daily Tar Heel* office to work as a freshman reporter. While his contemporaries were making friends and dating coeds in the best college tradition, Louis Kraar pounded away on his typewriter in the student newspaper office.

Later, as columnist and co-editor of the *Tar Heel*, he had taken it upon himself to be a defender of his University's best interests.

While everybody else was joining fraternities, he was prodding the frats for being too much apart from the rest of the campus.

While everybody else was flirting with student politics, he was prodding the politicians to stop talking so much and start doing something.

While everybody else was singing hallelujahs to the new football coach, he was wondering out loud if his coming didn't mean a new era for the University in which football would steamroller education.

Sometimes, of course, he was wrong. But he kept searching his conscience and writing accordingly.

Eventually, some of the students decided to swat the gadfly. They organized a recall election with the stated object of kicking Louis Kraar and his co-editor, Ed Yoder, out of office.

The election failed by a sizable margin, but Louis got the drift—a lot of people didn't like him.

Then, this week, he was persuaded to attend the tapping of the Golden Fleece, highest honorary organization on the campus, which adds a handful of students to its ranks each year in a dramatic public ceremony.

He didn't kid himself about his own chances for membership. Among the Golden Fleece members were several who had come within range of his barbs—and, as he knew, it took only two blackballs to keep him out.

That's why he was surprised when the thin spotlight suddenly snaked across the audience toward him, when the robed figure stalked to his side, gripped him by the shoulders and lifted him to his feet in an amplified voice spoke his name.

"Louis Kraar, Charlotte, North Carolina, Honor student. Devoted and tireless journalist. Courageous co-editor of *The Daily Tar Heel*. Identified with publications for one entire student generation."

The applause of his fellow students was deafening as he marched up the aisle to join the others on the stage.

Louis Kraar, who spent his college days writing what he believed instead of making friends, couldn't understand it all.

Bob Green Works On Theory Everyone Likes Good Hot Dog

April 30, 1956

E VERYBODY," Bob Green will tell you, "loves a good hot dog."

You stand in the tiny brick building on W. 4th St. near Mint St. (you HAVE to stand, because there isn't any place to sit) and watch Bob Green serve 'em up with that constant instinctive smile of his and you understand right away that when he talks about hot dogs, he knows what he's talking about.

Twelve hours a day for 30 years, Sundays and holidays and 18 months in the U.S. Army excepted, he's been dealing in hot dogs from the same old stand.

You'll never find Green's Lunch empty; partly, no doubt, because of the hot dogs ("There's nothing to it. I just put the steam to the buns and then use that premium grade weenie to set it off.") but also because his customers like to lean on the counter and talk to Bob about his new house and the family and to bask in the warmth of that inborn, incurable smile.

"I've made a lot of friends since 1926," Bob Green will tell you, "just doing nothing but selling hot dogs.

"The most my dad and I ever sold in a single day was 3,786 on a Christmas Eve. I don't know how many of them we ever got paid for—that was 1938 and we were on a credit system and about to go broke. We went into cash shortly after that."

All the time he's talking, he keeps turning away to wait on the customers who come through the swinging screen door and say, "Two all the way, Bob" or "One with sweet milk, Bob."

The customers come in a considerable variety. A stoop shouldered laborer stands beside a mailman from the Post Office up the street. They all get smiled upon, and they almost always smile back.

"I call this a 'hit and run' place," Bob says over his shoulder. "Before he died, Dad always said if you put stools into a little place like this, it would be too crowded. The people are mighty nice about it; they never complain."

Bob Green tells you this with three steaming franks in one hand, the other one deftly applying onions, mustard and ketchup in the reflex action of the trade.

"How's it going, Bob?" he'll get asked, and he'll lean on the counter long enough to say how it's going, smiling all the time.

"I'll tell you why people keep coming back," he says. "Everybody loves a good hot dog."

And that's partly the reason.

Also, everybody loves Bob Green.

May 1956

———

I remember when Charles came to work for the Charlotte News. *He was just this very young person with a lot of talent. I was six or eight years older than Charles, and even then he looked very young and very fresh. The most remarkable thing about him was his beautiful voice. He really belonged in the branch of journalism where people could hear him as well as read him. I think Charles had a great deal of feeling for the* Charlotte News, *because there had been a lot of talent on the paper historically, and he certainly fit into the pattern of the men and women who had worked there before. He always handled things in a very laid-back manner, never impressed with who he was. In his columns, Charles could make people very happy, and he could make people very sad, but he never became maudlin. He knew where to stop.*

—Anne Sawyer Cleland, *Charlotte News* reporter

Alice Newton Beats The Tom-Tom For Modern Dance In Charlotte

May 1, 1956

To the beat of a tom-tom, a petite, dark girl in tights swept her body through the room in the undulating movement of a wave breaking gently on the shore.

She rolled, like a wave, then relaxed, as a wave does, and dropped to the floor and slid slowly across it, just as a wave runs itself out on a broad beach.

She WAS a wave, taken from a painting of ocean waves on the Mint Museum gallery wall, where this curious business took place.

She was also a young Charlotte housewife with a love for modern dancing, and a student of Alice Newton.

Mrs. Newton, who had been beating the tom-tom, stopped to explain:

"This is a little different from other kinds of dancing. It's, well—more fluid and creative.

"Modern dancing is an expression of your own feeling or of the things around you. You have more freedom than in ballet, for example, because there are no set forms to follow.

"I come from Wisconsin, and this is my fourth year of teaching here, though I've lived in Charlotte for 10 years.

Most of the students are housewives. We do have one commercial artist and one Red Cross worker and one 11-year-old
girl—but no men this year. We usually have a couple of
men.

"One of the students, the one who was interpreting the
wave, studied at Bard College in New York. That's Eva. Janie
is a former ballet dancer. She has a hard time because she
keeps slipping back into ballet steps. There aren't any steps in
modern dancing.

"You can dance to anything—to an emotion, to a painting or piece of music or sculpture—and not just to the
forms as Eva did, but to the mood. Sometimes we interpret
Shakespeare sonnets, the words of the meter, and each dance
has a different interpretation, of course.

"Nobody has ever given much thought to eye-appeal,
to costuming, so modern dance isn't very popular with the
public. A stage full of leotards isn't much to look at. There are
signs of change, though. Someday, it may be as interesting to
watch as it is to dance."

Janie, a beautiful barefoot blonde, had picked out another
painting. The students watched her dance and studied the
paintings to try to guess which one she was interpreting, and
Mrs. Newton went back to beating the tom-tom.

Ted Kesterson, Super Locksmith, Never Met A Man Who Lost A Key

May 2 ,1956

Ted Kesterson travels 100,000 miles a year just getting people into and out of bathrooms, vaults, cars, buildings—and even, now and then, jails.

"And you know," he says, "I never met a man who lost a key. It's always 'My wife lost it,' or 'That no good clerk lost it.'

"I had a fellow come in this morning with a broken door-lock. He said, 'Somebody took this lock apart trying to fix it.'

"Nobody ever takes a lock apart himself. It's always somebody else who did it."

Mr. Kesterson, owner of Charlotte Safe & Lock Co., is the man the FBI calls when it wants a demonstration on expert locksmithing.

Lots of other people call on him too.

Like the mother of the little boy who got locked out of her kitchen last Christmas—with the family's turkey ablaze in the oven.

Or the manager of a locked building in New London, who found to his embarrassment that all his keys were lost.

Or the countless office workers who can't seem to remember the combination of the safe.

Or the relatives of an elderly, deaf lady, who had locked herself in her room for the sheer amusement of it.

Or the nurse in a local hospital whose emergency room door had snapped tight with a patient on the operating table.

Or—believe it or not—the jailer in Wadesboro whose most trusted trusty had just walked off the premises with all the keys.

Ted Kesterson is equal to all those situations.

"I never found a door I couldn't open," he says.

And does he pick locks with hairpins, or open combination safes with educated fingers that feel the tumblers drop?

"Nope," he snorts. "I usually use master keys, or chisels or dynamite.

"That educated fingers routine is good for one thing: settling down after your Saturday bath and watching on television."

O.R. Cobb Is A Young Man In Charge Of A Very Big Job

May 3, 1956

An INTERVIEW WITH O.R. COBB COMES HARD.

There's the pneumatic drill digging into the pavement outside his tiny office over the Church St. sidewalk.

His workers are manning the jackhammers, making the first tiny hole that will become a 15-story-home for Wachovia Bank by 1958.

So it goes like this:

WHACKETY - BAPBAPBAPBAPBAPBAPBAPBAP

"Right now, we're underpinning that building over there on Tryon St. It's going to be next door. It has a foundation already, of course, but if we dig down there beside it, it won't have one long.

"Sure (RATATATATATATATATATATATATA) I'm a little young. I left State College in 1950, but I've been on some big projects since (TATATATATAT) hope to have my 30th birthday right here in December.

"We're going down about 20 feet and then we'll start going up (TATATATATATATAT) beams, columns and slabs through the 15th floor.

"I'm what's called the 'job engineer.' It's mostly a job of

keeping ahead of everybody else (KAPOWKAPOWKAPOW) layout work, spotting, you know.

"That roof over the sidewalk is to keep nuts and bolts and things off people's heads. We're painting the whole barricade, because it's going to be here a long time and it's in the middle of the city and ought to look good (BAMBAMBAMBAMBAMB AMBAMBAMBAM).

"We cut some pretty good-sized peepholes for people who want to watch, too.

"Sorry this office (BAMTATATATATA) more comfortable. That's a little trick of the trade. It's supposed to be big enough for me—convenient but not comfortable, so people won't come up here to (POWPOWPOWPOWPOWPOW) and loaf.

"I'm really looking forward to this. It's a beautiful (D-R-R-R-R-R-R-R) building and I hope you'll (D-R-R-R-R-R-R-R-R) and see us again some time."

Dick Pitts Causes Trouble For Dick Pitts, And Vice Versa

May 4, 1956

W E'LL TRY TO KEEP THIS SIMPLE.

There are two Dick Pittses, see, the public relations one at the Carolina Motor Club and the parking garage one on W. 4th St.

They are not even distant cousins.

But try to convince the public.

Dick Pitts (the parking one) gets downright plaintive about it.

"I'm just a plain old automobile storage man," he says. "I've lived here for 21 years."

But that never made any difference to the folks whose daughter, maybe, was in a Little Theater play and got a panning from Dick Pitts (the public relations one) back when he was a newspaper critic.

"They used to cuss me out," says Parking Pitts. "Me! I never even heard of their daughter."

"I met him one time and apologized to him," says Public Relations Pitts.

"Yes, but there's nothing he could do about it. Nothing I could do about it either," says Parking Pitts.

Then Public Relations Pitts left town, went to New York and Chicago—far enough away for Parking Pitts to breathe a sigh of relief and settle down to being Charlotte's one and only Dick Pitts. Things were calm, and unconfused, and peaceful.

"Until one day a guy shook my hand and said he saw in the paper where I was starting an automobile safety campaign," Parking Pitts laments. "I knew that fellow was back in town."

"It was my campaign," Public Relation Pitts says. "And about that time a fellow came up and asked me how my garage was getting along."

Eager to help, we present here a simple photo-guide. Dick Pitts and Dick Pitts, reading from left to right.

Or, come to think of it, from right to left.

Cy Rainwater Has A Heart As Big As The Cab He Drives

May 7, 1956

T HERE ARE SOME WHO SAY a lifetime of dealing with the public will harden a man and make him cynical about human nature, but it hasn't worked out that way for Cy Rainwater.

Cy is a bronzed man with a wrinkled face and a heart as big as the taxicab he drives.

There's nobody but Cy, no wife or family, and so he adopted the whole town as sort of a proving ground for a hunch he

had: that it is more blessed to give than receive, and more fun, too.

Every Sunday, he takes a fare or two to church, to big

churches or to little ones, and he gives them all a dollar bill to put in the plate for him.

Some of the customers are right surprised at this, but they all take the money and Cy feels fairly certain they all put it in the plate.

Churches are not the only recipients of Cy's dollar bills, either. He doesn't like to talk about it, but a lot of his fellow cab drivers know.

They remember, for example, the time last winter when he was parked over on A. St. and noticed a Negro woman walking around collecting scraps of wood.

Now that you mention it, Cy remembers that. "Well, I knew just what she was doing," he says. "She was picking up wood for the stove. So I just gave her a dollar and told her to go buy some wood."

And how about the blind man in tattered clothes last week?

"Well, I just pulled over and gave him a dollar, too.

"See, I don't give to the Red Cross or anything like that. I run into a lot of people who look like they could use a dollar, and so I give them one.

"I don't do it for the publicity or the Christianity of it. I don't want to act like I'm something I'm not. It just gives me a good feeling."

It all started with his grandmother and granddaddy back home in Rockingham.

"They always told me to help anybody less fortunate than I was, and I don't believe they told me wrong," Cy says.

Giving to churches is part of that, giving to blind and crippled people is part, buying wood for a woman who doesn't have any wood of her own is part.

It just gives Cy Rainwater a good feeling.

A.B. Medlin, 87, Is Still Trapping Minks In Mecklenburg

May 8, 1956

A.B. MEDLIN IS AN 87-YEAR-OLD Mecklenburg County fur trapper.

That's the simple truth of it, and if you didn't think Mecklenburg County had any fur trappers, that just shows you don't know A.B. Medlin.

He'll sit down on the front porch of the little house on Beattys Ford Rd., the house he built himself, and tell you about his years as a trapper.

"Minks," he'll say.

"That's what I try to get. I've caught 'em right up in the city limits. But this past winter was no count, Mister. I didn't get but three minks.

"I got lots of gray foxes, and one red fox, and let me see ... more coons and possums than I can count, and plenty of Muskrats, and dogs, oh, Lord, the dogs I did catch, Mister ... "

Minks? Muskrats? In Mecklenburg County?

"Well, there ain't as many minks as there used to be," he'll tell you. "I've cleaned 'em out."

He'll sit there on the porch rail, cross one tall boot over the other one, and tell you how it's done:

"Mister Mink is a smart animal. There's just one habit of his that gets him in trouble, and it's this: If he goes up a stream today, he'll come back tomorrow.

"Now if you see where he's gone up the stream, you can put that trap between the stream bank and an old tree, and when he comes back down the stream—Bangyow!—you've got yourself a mink."

It's even easier than that with muskrats and possums, Mr. Medlin says. And as for the "sly" fox:

"I can catch Mister Fox just as quick as I can catch a dog."

Many times, Mr. Medlin has thought about going to Florida or to the mountains to do his trapping.

"But Florida's too doggone hot and the mountains are too doggone hilly."

So he stays in Mecklenburg.

"There's hardly a stream, pond, lake or river around here. I haven't trapped, Mister," he'll tell you.

"I'll string those traps out maybe two, three miles and I'll walk that trap line every single day. I'll catch something. It won't be a mink every day—though I caught 19 in the winter of 1948—but I'll catch me something.

"Then I'll skin it and pack the pelt in a box and when the box gets full, I'll ship 'er off to Taylor Fur Co. in St. Louis, Mo.—I've been dealing with Taylor for 40 years—and then back'll come a little money."

The trapping season is over now and Mr. Medlin has settled down to gardening in a plot beside his house.

For the first time in years, he's got somebody to keep him company until the winter rolls around again.

"Her name's Mary," he says. "I got her over in Charlotte. She's not quite as old as I am, but she's interested in trapping and I like her fine. We got married two months ago."

Bob Gillis Wields A Pretty Flashy Sword

May 9, 1956

BOB GILLIS NEVER JUMPED ON A HOLLYWOOD TABLE and hacked down a chandelier in his life, but he wields a pretty flashy sword, just the same.

He does it at weekly YMCA classes for chemical engineers, ad men and housewives who want to learn swordplay from an expert.

Bob, a former Southern champion who works as a manufacturer's representative, has a piece of advice for his saber pupils: "Whatever's sticking out, you slug it."

It's more subtle than that with the other two weapons in the fencer's arsenal, the foil, a long, limber, blunt-tipped instrument, and the epee, a stiff, sharp dueling weapon.

"But with the saber," Bob says, "you just put your hand on your hip and hack away. The saber goes back to cavalry days. A good saber match is like a tap-dance, with sparks.

"The whole thing is to be more mental than physical. You have to be agile, but the main thing is thinking ahead. It's not always true that a good big man can beat a good little man.

"There are three schools, Italian, Spanish and French. I teach the French method because it's the only one I know very much about.

"Fencing is like an international fraternity. It was like a passport into Mexico when I went down there. All the military and government people fence in Mexico.

"It's catching on very well in Charlotte. I have 20 students, more than I could ever find in Atlanta. We hope to form a fencing club someday.

"They teach it in high schools in New York, and the American Theater Wing makes all its students take lessons for poise and grace and for any Shakespearean plays that come along.

"Fencing goes back to the Renaissance, I think, but it's made some strides. They have an electronic epee now that rings a bell whenever a point is scored. You have to know what you're doing with the epee. It's made of tempered steel, always European steel, and it's stiff. If you lunge too hard ... well, you have to be careful. Women don't use the epee.

"Women make good fencers, though, often better than men. We have a few married couples in my classes and if the wives learn faster than the husbands, it makes for complications sometimes.

"A new fencer can start getting full enjoyment out of the sport in four to six months. Good fencers are often 50 to 60 years old. Age really has no bearing once you get into it.

"Look at Erroll Flynn."

John Black Lives In A World Of Tachometers And Gymkhanas

May 10, 1956

T HE WORLD OF JOHN BLACK IS A WORLD OF TACHOMETERS, computers and gymkhanas, of piston displacement and revolutions per minute.

As *major domo* of Imperial Motors, he is adviser, friend, salesman and father confessor to foreign car owners all over the Carolinas.

They make the shop behind his W. Morehead St. showroom their personal rally grounds on Saturday afternoons, rolling in from miles away in Jaguars, MG's and Austin-Healeys for the privilege of sitting around and jawing with each other—about Jaguars, MG's and Austin-Healeys.

A special event, like the sports car climb of Chimney Rock last month, furnishes the brotherhood conversational fodder for weeks. They're still talking about why it was Glaspar instead of a Jag that got to the top of the hill first.

The more they talk, the more John Black sells and services.

"No doubt about it," he says, "sports cars are booming. We've got about 70 in Charlotte right now. Doctors own nine of them. Newspapermen own maybe five or six, lawyers and radio-television people own a dozen, or more. That accounts for about a third, right there."

He leans back in his office, cluttered with stop-clocks, photographs and signal flags, and gives it to you straight.

"I'm a red-blooded American, but let's face it: Driving an American car is like driving a bus. There's just no comparison in the 'feel,' the handling ability ...

"Some people will do anything to get one. I've traded for two airplanes, a cow, a motorcycle and all kinds of cars. Once you drive an MG, say, or a Jaguar XK-140, you're hooked."

To domestic-trained drivers switching to sports cars, he gives you one piece of advice: "If you're not ready to turn, don't turn the wheel, and if you're not ready to go, don't step on the gas."

And having made this racy declaration, he'll tell you something else: "I don't drive a sports car myself.

"I have a little Morris out there, a foreign car but not technically a sports car. It gets 30 miles to the gallon, that's what I like about it.

"But I go to all the rallies and the races on these abandoned airstrips. I don't race, I'm too old, but it's something to see ...

"Sports car owners just love to talk. I'll tell you that. And if they can brag about their cars, if they're meeting each other on the highway or something, they'll always throw up their hands and blow their horns.

"That tells a lot about foreign car ownership right there. They're all members of a brotherhood."

And John Black is big brother.

Sadness And Anger Nailed Out In The House That Paul Built

May 11, 1956

P AUL BUILT A HOUSE.

It is made of old two-by-fours and cast-off plywood and it sits in the back yard of Alexander Home.

It is not a perfect house, not a very pretty one, but it was built by Paul, and that is something to be considered.

When he came to the home two years ago, Paul had no inclination toward building houses. Nobody had ever taught him to drive a nail or saw a board.

Paul didn't understand such a thing as love, in which the home is rich. When the games started, he often sat by himself, sad and angry.

It was about last Christmas when he first said, "I want to build a house." The boys at the home had talked about building a house before, but they had never gotten around to it.

Paul repeated it a few days later: "I want to build a house."

There was something in his voice, something in the firmness of it, a hint in the look of his face, that made people at the home start looking around for scrap lumber.

A church furnished some, a lumber company furnished some more, and some nails and a hammer.

They gave it all to Paul. In a few days, they heard him in the back yard, driving a nail.

He worked every day, driving more nails, sawing the boards to fit, or almost fit. He used cardboard for the roof, but when it rained the cardboard got soggy, so he replaced it with planks to cover the tarpaper.

The others stood watching while Paul walked around inside the house, putting down a floor. It wasn't long before he put them to work, too, and every boy in the home was out there working on Paul's house.

They used up the lumber on two rooms. They needed more, and the home found some more for them. They tore out one wall and added two more rooms.

Paul directed it all. He found some hinges and made a door himself, and when he put it on the house, it swung as well as any door.

The house has been finished for three weeks now. The boys have painted "NO GIRLS" on it and they use it to play cowboys and Indians.

Sadness and anger were somehow nailed outside the four walls and the tarpaper roof.

Paul is one of the cowboys.

Bob Raiford Is Among 'The Men That Don't Fit In'

May 14, 1956

H E TOLD HIS LISTENERS THAT HE HAD GONE OUT ON THE STREET and recorded some opinions on the attack on Nat "King" Cole the night before in Birmingham, Ala., and that the station had ordered him not to play the tapes on the air.

He played one of the tapes, an interview with Chief of Police Frank Littlejohn, and then went on talking.

"You can't keep everything under your hat," he said. "I'm no rabble-rouser, no integrationist, either, but you can't keep everything under your hat."

They ordered him off the air at 11 a.m. and fired him the next day.

Thinking about it, he said, "WBT's a good place to work. It's a secure place, too."

Security wasn't enough, either.

"Maybe," he said, "it's a little too secure for a 28-year-old in a business as static as this one is.

"I don't blame them for firing me, of course. I expected it, and they came in on cue. I see the station is still on the air, and I'll live as long."

So he went to New York, walked the soles out on a pair of

shoes, and got a job at NBC.

Is NBC any less secure?

"I don't know," Bob Raiford says. "They have a lot of imagination there. I'm very hopeful."

Announcing wasn't enough, the shows weren't enough, security wasn't what Bob Raiford was looking for. He could never work a nine to five job. No mold he's found exactly fits him.

It's not exactly wanderlust that's got him, not precisely revolt that's in him.

New York may be just what he's looking for.

But they even work nine to five jobs in New York, and in that case, what is a man to do?

Dave Staton: North Charlotte Took Its Troubles To His Door

May 15, 1956

Y OU DIDN'T KNOW HIM?" Mrs. Lydia Brooks could hardly believe it.

"I just feel like everybody knew him," she said.

He was a grocer. But to the people who live 30 blocks out N. Caldwell St. and on the streets to either side, David Staton was more than that.

The sign outside stills says "D.C. Staton Grocery" and inside, Guy Suddreth, who went to work for Mr. Staton when he was eight years old, will lean against the check-out counter and tell you about him.

"People came to him for everything," he says. "Uncle Dave got us a fire station out here and helped get 36th St. widened. Some people call him 'the mayor of Charlotte' ...

"He loved North Charlotte, and nobody better say anything against it.

"One time some ladies came in here, dressed fancy, campaigning for a man for judge. One of them said, 'Of course, we don't want the mill vote.' Uncle Dave just asked them to get out of here ... "

You can walk up the street to Dorton Drug Store and talk

to J.D. Dover.

"I knew him for 22 years," he'll tell you. "He was a mighty nice fellow. He kept lots of people on the books at the store and never collected from them.

"During one strike, down here at Highland Mill, he kept some children from starving. I know that. He stuck by people all the time ... "

Darce Mullis, who runs the Service Grill, knew David Staton, too.

"I went to work for him at his cafe, before he ever opened the grocery store. I was about 10 years old. He carried me to town three or four times a year and dressed me from head to foot.

"He started me off right and we always stuck together, even after I worked a notice and went out on my own. If I ever had a problem, he'd help me with it. He's done it for many boys, but I believe I was closest to him. He was about the best man I've ever known."

Mr. Staton died last week. The honorary pallbearers at his funeral were Henry A. Yancy, Col. Paul Younts, Frank N. Littlejohn, Claude Albea, Herbert H. Baxter, Steve Dellinger, Clyde Hunter, Grady Cole, Basil Boyd, Sid Y. McAden, J. Lester Wolfe, Ben Douglas, T.W. Church and Harold Pierce—all friends, and people whose names you know.

But there were hundreds of other friends whose names you may never have heard. They were the people of North Charlotte, David Staton's people.

Mrs. Brooks spoke for all of them.

"There are not too many like him out this way, I'll tell you that."

Francis O'Clee Finds Charlotte Has Little Shipbuilding Work

May 16, 1956

THE COUNTRYSIDE AROUND RAMSGATE, KENT, on the south shore of England turns green in May. The little town by the sea is at its most beautiful.

Out on Tuckaseegee Rd., in the apartment of his daughter and son-in-law, Francis O'Clee is remembering Ramsgate. He grew up there, married there and became a welder on the steel sides of ships that sailed up to the chalky cliffs and into Ramsgate's harbor.

He's still a welder, and that's the trouble.

When his daughter, Margaret, and Calvin Estridge, the Charlotte Air Force man she had met and married, invited Mr. and Mrs. O'Clee to Charlotte to live, he assumed there would be plenty of new steel in Charlotte that would need a master welder's touch.

But there isn't. Charlotte is not an industrial city. There are no ship's sides that need welding. Francis O'Clee hasn't picked up a mask or a torch in the seven weeks he's been here.

"I started looking right away," he says. "I spent a day or two seeing the sights, and then I went out to find a job.

"I went to the labor exchange and then to all the steel and engineering companies. They all say they are waiting for orders, or something of the sort. No luck, so far."

It's not a question of needing a job to feed the family, as it is with many people out of work. It's just that Francis O'Clee is a welder, not a man who enjoys reading magazines or watching television. He likes the feel of the mask on his face, he likes the look of a good seam weld.

"I don't know what to do with myself," he says.

"We used to do all sorts of work at home—work on the old tugs that came down from the Thames, and work on the Admiralty ships. The Navy steel was good and strong, you know, and you could do a good job on it."

Francis O'Clee crossed the sea he grew up beside to start a new life, leaving his home and his craft behind. He expected to regain at least one of the two.

Ramsgate is green in his memory. Charlotte, where they don't have any Thames, or tugs, or Navy steel, is gray.

Israel Smith Collects Junk By Day, Plays Violin At Night

May 17, 1956

ISRAEL SMITH TRUDGES AROUND ALL DAY AMID MOUNTAINS OF IRON that rise 50 feet above the ground of his junk yard on S. Graham St.

All day long, Israel Smith listens to the clanging, clattering cranes dropping their magnets and grapples into fantastic heaps of bed springs, automobile bodies, oil drums, axles, milk cans and stoves.

He listens to the bailing press smash piles of scrap iron flat. He listens to thousands of pipe fittings clanking into freight cars.

Then, at night, he goes home and plays his violin.

Israel Smith is a junkman with a soul. He has been buying "iron, brass and rags from dealers, plants and peddlers, off trucks, trains and handcarts" for almost 30 years. For much of that time, he has also been playing violin in the Charlotte Symphony Orchestra.

He likes Mozart better than scrap iron, and there was a time, after he left New York's Julliard School of Music in 1928, when he flirted with the idea of becoming a concert violinist.

"But there's no money in Mozart," he says. There is money in piles of lamp bases, garage roofs and airplane motors.

So during the day, Israel Smith keeps his Guadagnini violin in its case and puts up with the banging, clanking and clattering.

All through the day, he's dreaming of the night.

Of Addenda And Conclusions, Secretaries And Black Sheep

May 18, 1956

AT WEEK'S END, time to chase down some addendas, conclusions and corrections on recent "People":

Remember Martha Farmer, the Hampton, Va., secretary who fell in love over a chocolate milkshake in the Charlotte bus station?

No happy ending here. Martha and the man of her dreams exchanged photographs and wrote to each other for a couple of weeks.

He said he wanted to come to Virginia to see her, but he never did.

"I still hope he might," Martha said this week—but with the inflection of a lonely girl who doesn't really believe it.

Thomas J. Hunter's dream was a different sort.

He wanted a black sheep.

He had searched the Carolinas over, but he couldn't find one.

A Kingstree, S.C., farmer read his story in *The News*.

He had a black sheep.

Thomas J. Hunter has him now.

A postcard comes in the mail from the Rev. Shelton

Hutchison, the amazing preacher who plays 20 musical instruments, manufactures yardsticks, reads Hebrew and Greek, fishes, plays golf, lectures and debates and collects fossils, minerals, coins, buttons, antiques, music, boxes and coats of arms.

A postcard—from Canada, first stop on a 'round-the-world tour for the preacher who never gets tired.

"There's a race of men that don't fit in,
"A race that can't stay still;
"So they break the hearts of kith and kin,
"And they roam the world at will."

That's the first stanza of a poem we used to describe Bob Raiford, the disc jockey who got fired. It fits. It was not written by Rudyard Kipling, either, as many, many fans of Robert W. Service have noted.

It seems Dick Pitts (the parking garage operator) and Dick Pitts (the Carolina Motor Club publicist) aren't the only two men in town whose names get confused.

J.B. Clark, WBT's Carolinas news director, called to tell about the telephone calls he gets at all hours from folks who really mean to be calling J.B. Clark (the city police officer) or J.B. Clark (the state highway patrolman) or J.B. Clark (the workman at Highland Park Manufacturing Co.)

And Mrs. Tom Sawyer, 2235 Shenandoah Ave., wants the world to know her husband is not a radio executive—and definitely not Tom Sawyer, the candidate for governor.

So? So they all ought to be glad they aren't named James (46 in Charlotte) or John (53) Smith.

George Is Back, And Everybody Is Happy Again On E. 4th St.

May 21, 1956

T HE PEOPLE WHO WORK IN THE OFFICES AND STORES in the first block of E. 4th. St. tried to persuade George Anton not to leave.

They'd sit on the stools in Anton's Grill and tell him, "Look, George, you've been here seven years. You've built this place up from nothing ... " or "George, you're running the best grill anywhere around here. You don't want to go now ... "

But George had his eye on bigger things. He'd shake his head and tell them, "A fellow's got to move on if he's ever going to get anywhere."

He'd say, "Look, eight stools and three little booths. What kind of place is that?"

Last month, the big offer came. It was so good George couldn't turn it down. He sold out and went to work in a big restaurant on Morehead St.

It was a good job—eight hours a day for a change, and he liked it at first. He had time to go fishing, time to work around the house, time to be with his wife and new daughter.

But every now and then, he'd run into one of his old customers, and the customer would say, "George, it's not the same since you left. The coffee's gone way down, boy ... " or "This new guy, he doesn't even play the ball games on the radio, George."

He kept trying to make a go of the new job. He had ambition. But he got homesick.

So George Anton walked down to E. 4th St. last week. He stood outside the grill for a minute. Then he walked in and bought it back.

The coffee's good again, the ball game is going on the radio, there's a big sign on the window.

It says, "George Is Back!"

"Fellow across the street painted it and wouldn't charge me a thing," George says. "What do you know about that?"

Eight stools, three little booths and George. Everybody's happy.

Barbara Bamberger, Age 12, Wants To Act Role Of Antigone

May 22, 1956

W hat," inquired the old guy with his foot on the rail and his hand curled around the beer glass, "is the Younger Generation coming to?"

Well, that's an old and honored question, Mac. You ought to know Barbara Bamberger.

Twelve years old, Mac. T-w-e-l-v-e years old. Daughter of Mr. and Mrs. E.J. Bamberger, 1431 Scotland Ave. Goes to Eastover School.

She gave an acting demonstration to the Woman's Club the other day. Real good. Let her tell you:

"I've played Dorothy in 'The Wizard of Oz' and Peter Pan in 'Peter Pan,' and, gosh, I don't know. Mrs. Masterson (of Masterson Theater School, her teacher) counted up and I've played 60 or 70 parts."

Okay, Mac, so maybe you WERE the dice champ of the sixth grade when you were in school. Were you smart as a whip, cute as a button, and talented? Except at rolling sevens?

"My favorite actor is Fess Parker, only I don't like him as Davy Crockett. I don't like cowboys and things. The part I'd really like to play is 'Medea' or maybe 'Antigone.' "

Medea and Antigone. By Euripides and Sophocles, Mac. You probably never heard of them when you were 12 years old. You probably never heard of them yet.

"I had a demonstration for third graders the other day. Murder! They didn't understand to well.

"I practice emotions, too. You know—joy, despair, horror and all."

Admit it, Mac. When you were a kid, joy was something that came from smoking rabbit tobacco cigarettes. Despair was when your Daddy caught you.

"I want to be an actress when I grow up, but if I can't make it, I'd like to be a librarian or a paleontologist."

Boy, there's one for you, Mac. Roll that "paleontologist" around. Look it up in the dictionary, and if you can figure out how to spell it, you'll find it means somebody who studies dinosaurs and old bones.

Speaking of which, how's your arthritis, Mac?

Pinky Tells About Naming Buck, Puddin', Pokey, Bippy

May 23, 1956

M RS. PHIL VAN EVERY HAD A BEAUTIFUL NAME WHEN SHE WAS A GIRL: Carolyn.

So her Daddy called her "Pinky."

"I resolved," she says, "if I ever had any daughters, they'd never get a nickname."

She has four daughters—named "Buck," "Puddin'," "Pokey," and "Bippy."

Lots of people think they don't have any other names. If you ask their father (His Honor The Mayor), he'll tell you as much. But His Honor's wife is at least as reliable a source as His Honor, and she claims it was all a conspiracy that happened like this:

"When Buck—I mean, Mary Lance—was born," Mrs. Van Every says, "Phil thought sure it was going to be a boy. We named her Mary Lance, but he called her 'Buck.' "

A couple of years later, along came Carolyn.

"He was SURE she was going to be a boy," Mrs. Van Every remembers. "We named her Carolyn—but he called her 'Pete.' "

That's where the second conspirator came in. The cook

decided Carolyn was too sweet to be Pete. She called her "Puddin'." Who is a mother to hang on to "Carolyn" in a spot like that? "Puddin' " stuck.

Three years later, Anne was born. The family expected her Aug. 22, Puddin's birthday. August 22 came and went. No Anne. She was born Aug. 23. The mayor was equal to the occasion. Annie became "Pokey."

Diana almost escaped. Mr. Van Every didn't nickname her. Mrs. Van Every certainly didn't. The cook stayed out of it.

So Mary Lance—"Buck"—came skipping home from school one day, scooped baby Diana up in her arms and said, "Hi Bippy."

Diana became Bippy.

Pinky surrendered.

Frank Raborn Has One Arm, But That's Enough For Banjo

May 24, 1956

W ELL, MY NAME IS FRANK RABORN. I was 75 years old last New Year's Day, and I can dance a buck dance yet!"

He's an old man with a battered hat and a banjo. He has only one arm.

"That's all I need. I hit them strings with four fingers, and I can make 'John Henry' walk and talk!"

He has a regular schedule: First Presbyterian Church Monday and Tuesday, St. Mark's Wednesday and Thursday, across the street from the YMCA Friday, Sears-Roebuck on Saturday.

"I come over from Thomasboro on the bus. That tin box is my treasure. I never ask for money, and I get more than them that does."

The sound he gets from the banjo is an old sound and a quiet sound, and sometimes he sings along under his breath:

"Hark, hark, old Joe Clark,

"Dance, Miss Betsy Brown,

"If I don't get the girl I want

"I'm going to leave this town."

"I didn't get the girl, though. I was going to marry her Sunday, and she died Thursday. That was 52 years ago, and I ain't left yet!"

He laughs at that, and when he laughs, his eyes close tight, and when he stops laughing, his eyes are looking way back down the years.

"I married another girl, you see, and raised a family, seven children, five living. I swept the cotton mill, hoed, picked cotton. I could do anything. I could chop a cord of wood a day, and that was just a light task.

"They turned me out of the mill because I had a gray hair, and I took to playing the banjo."

His knuckles are smooth from age, but his fingers are limber when they dance on the strings.

"I can play all the old time music, 'Sally Goodin', 'Sally Ann,' 'Shortenin' Bread,' 'Long Leaf Pine,' 'Betty Brown,' 'Reuben' ... The people are always stopping to listen and that old-time music does 'em so much good, sometimes they just about have to dance ...

"One time, a man gave me a $20 bill. I kept waiting around for him to come back, but he never did, and I went on down to Carolina Beach and had a big time. I made another $20 down there and I come on back.

"I don't drink whisky and I go to church, but I would like to get to Carolina Beach just one more time before I die ...

"If I get there, it'll be the same way I've got everything for the past 25 years, playing this banjo."

He cocks his head, and he bends it over the strings. Don't talk to him when he's picking, because he won't hear you.

Sung Nak Pil: 'It Shall Never Be Forgotten'

May 25, 1956

I HAVE WHAT I ALWAYS WANTED," the letter begins, "with the help of good, warm-hearted Americans, who helped me as they do for their own children or brothers ... "

The Americans who helped Sung Nak Pil are people who read his story in *The Charlotte News* two months ago, when he was trying to raise the $100 entrance fee of the University of Pusan, Korea.

They read the words of ex-GI Jack Pentes, a Charlotte commercial artist who knew him in Korea.

"One of the most brilliant guys I've ever known," Jack Pentes called him, "and one of the poorest."

The Americans read all that, and they took up a collection at a Charlotte filling station, they kicked in at the weekly meeting of the Cramerton Kiwanis Club, they dug into their own pockets.

The Americans gave the money to Jack Pentes and he sent it all to Pusan. It got there the day registration closed, just in time.

Back came the letter:

"How could I ever think about I could be helped by the

people who are more than 10,000 miles away, over the Pacific and farthest part of America from here, and they've helped whom has not seen and is not more than a boy ... "

The money was enough to put Sung Nak Pil into school. Then came the job of keeping him there.

He earned a little money himself while studying French, English and German and a half-dozen other courses—and his friends hocked their watches for him but it wasn't enough.

Something, Jack Pentes figured, had to be done. The letter was on his mind:

"I am so sorry to be helped from the people who lost their young sons in the war to save my country. I like very much to serve for America, like they did for me, to repay their kindness ... "

So Jack Pentes took his letter to the Charlotte Junior Chamber of Commerce, and read it.

Day before yesterday, the Jaycees voted. They voted to set up the Subcommittee for the Sung Nak Pil Education Fund to keep him in clothes and books, and to send him $50 a month.

Members of the committee are Jack Pentes, Jim Radermacher, Ernie Hicks, Jim Sangster, Leon Gibbs, Andy Sealey and Franc White. They don't know where the money is coming from. But they know it must come from somewhere, because of the letter:

"I think some day I'll see Charlotte. I think I can.

"I owe Americans too much.

"Americans changed pathway of my life.

"It shall never be forgotten."

In Which Miss Buice Gives Traveler A Tip

May 28, 1956

THE VISITING NEWSPAPERMAN WALKED into Miss Vivian Buice's office at the Carolina Motor Club with a far away look in his eyes.

"Tell me about Tangier," he said. "Rhapsodize about Rome, Rangoon and the Riviera. Sing to me of Sorrento."

"Sit down," Miss Buice said. "What seems to be your trouble?"

"You are the manager of the World Travel Service, are you not?" the visitor inquired. "I long to roam."

"You are not alone," Miss Buice said. "This is the season, of course. I'd say 2,000 people are going to Europe this summer from right around here."

Into the desk, and out with the travel folders.

"They're going everywhere and for every reason. Most are tourists. Some are students. Some are Englishmen going back to England for a visit and Greeks going back to Greece.

"One couple is going to Russia, now that Russia's open. Awfully expensive in Russia. There are about four rubles to the dollar, and it takes 200 rubles to get a good dinner.

"Another couple is going on safari from Capetown to

Cairo. That will be hot.

"The people I'm most interested in, though, are those who are touring on a shoestring. Around the world on a freighter, doesn't that sound exciting?"

The visitor sat there open-mouthed. He was walking down the Champs Elysees, his pockets jingling with centimes, drachmas and rupees.

"Of course," Miss Buice said, "some people are bored with the Champs Elysees. They've been to all the conventional places. They're going to Australia, South America—have to watch out for the revolutions in South America—and odd little islands.

"Some space is opening up in the South Pacific—Honolulu, Fiji and New Zealand, and already it's hard to book passage."

The visitor leaned forward.

"That's for me," he said. "Glamour and romance, enchanting calypso rhythms, the radiant beauty of semi-tropical foliage beside the blue sea, sweeping pink sandy beaches ... "

Miss Buice interrupted him. "How much would you like to spend?" she asked.

The newspaperman whispered in her ear. "Well," she said, "let's see. Glamour ... Blue seas ... Sandy beaches ... "

She handed him a travel folder for his very own.

"Fun in the Sun," the folder said, "at Myrtle Beach."

Fighting Guerrillas In Greece Proved To Be Good Basic Training For Jimmie's New Occupation

May 29, 1956

JIMMIE POURLOS LEARNED HOW TO STAY CALM UNDER FIRE as a 16-year-old Greek rifleman fighting the Communist guerrillas in 1948.

It was a good, helpful lesson. It comes in handy every morning at 11:10.

Jimmie edges well to the rear of his Central Drive-In at that hour, cool as a cucumber. His waitresses, who never fought any Communists, bite their lips nervously and look at the clock.

There's a deep, deathly silence.

Then the door crashes open and 250 Central High School students race inside, hollering orders. The juke box starts. Everybody's laughing and talking about singing and dancing.

It's an unholy din.

What's Jimmie Pourlos doing? He's serving up 75 hamburgers, 60 hot dogs, 100 orders of French fries, two dozen hams on rye, making change, mixing Cokes, clearing off booths. He's not even breathing fast.

Then a bell rings, everybody rushes out, the juke box runs down, everything gets quiet again.

At 11:55, the next wave hits, at 12:50, another one. The counter's so thick you couldn't lay a razor down on it. The sound threshold is several decibels above eardrum-splitting level.

Jimmie Pourlos is smiling and chewing gum.

How does he do it?

"I don't think about the noise," he says. "I think about how lucky I am—28 years old and owner of a restaurant—or how I'm going to be an American citizen after a while ...

"I serve maybe 500 to 600 sandwiches in three hours every day. All through the summer, too, because they have summer school at Central.

"It gets pretty frantic in here and I used to get excited, but I'm just used to it now, that's all. The kids are wonderful ... "

He gets interrupted by the door crashing open. The kids. It's 2:45 and school's out. The juke box cranks up again.

"Hey, I even like rock 'n' roll music," Jimmie says. "It's cool."

Like Jimmie.

Watching Trains May Be Pastime For Some; But It's A Full-Time Job For Clarence Walker

May 30, 1956

A LOT OF PEOPLE LIKE TO WATCH THE TRAINS GO BY. Clarence Walker has dedicated his life to it.

For 35 years, he has sat in the two-story watchtower at the Southern railroad crossing on W. Trade St. like the conscience of the city.

He has sat there and looked down the tracks, hour after hour, with a single purpose.

"To hear that train when it comes and then to ring that bell and lower the gates on the crossing in the proper way and in ample time."

You'd think after 35 years Clarence Walker might figure he knows his job pretty well and that he might read a magazine or listen to the radio, sitting up there above the street.

But all he does is sit erect on an old horse-hair engineer's bench and keep his eyes trained on the rails that stretch beneath him.

"In this job," he'll tell you, "a man doesn't have time for nothing except just to remember his duty."

Clarence Walker's duty begins at 6 a.m. He lowers the gates for four passenger trains, 136 going north at 7 a.m.; 36

going north at 7:40; the southbound 29 at 8:20 and number 88 going south at 12:10.

In between, there are switch engines, freights and motor cars, and he lowers the gates for them all.

"First, I start the bell to ringing. I ring it by hand. It's a bell off a steam engine that was put here on the side of the tower in about 1940. The old bell tanged right keenly, but this one is louder.

"Then I let the gates down, the gates in the main traffic lane first. Every now and then, a car will stop on the track and go to see-sawing. Then I raise the gates enough for it to get under and holler to 'em to move on off.

"A lot of them will try to get under the gate or run through the open space after it's down. I've even had cars run into trains, but that was a long time ago.

"They added the 5th St. crossing to me at 12 o'clock the first of May this year. It's one block away down there and I just hit a switch to let those new gates down and then I turn my main attention to these here.

"If the power ever goes off, I have a whistle and a red lantern and I climb down and stop traffic in the street.

"Most of the time, though, my job is to just sit here and not miss anything that comes down the tracks."

Clarence Walker has watched a lot of things change since he first climbed up the ladder to the tower in 1919. The streets have changed, the traffic and the people and the buildings on them have changed.

The tower and the tracks have not changed, and neither has Clarence Walker's view of his job:

"To hear that train when it comes and then to ring that bell."

Want To Meet A Craftsman?
Mention Glass To Ralph Shoe

May 31, 1956

ALL THE LEARNED JOURNALS ARE COMPLAINING THESE DAYS about the decline of craftsmanship. The thesis is that television, sports cars, Cinerama, comic books and jet airliners have speeded the world to such a pace and drained its time and attention to such a degree that the old-time craftsman who is proud of his work is gone forever.

This is a large and windy thesis. Take no stock in it.

Even in modernistic trades, there are people who know how to do their jobs very well, indeed.

Take Ralph Shoe. Ralph Shoe knows about glass. He has installed it in window-pane size and in sheets 14-feet square, at ground level in the Coliseum and in an airport control tower 90 feet in the air.

You want to meet a man who loves his job? Get Ralph Shoe talking about glass.

"After Hurricane Hazel," he'll tell you, "we had a real shortage of glass. Everybody wanted it, because it blew out of almost every window on the coast and right through the eastern part of the state. We (that's Pritchard Paint & Glass Co.) can fill the demand, now.

"This is a pretty dangerous business. A fellow dropped a big pane coming out of a railroad car the other day and got cut bad. The big thing is to be careful. You're putting a big pane in, maybe 170 inches—that's the biggest we handle in stock—and if you tighten one screw a speck too much, you've lost yourself a glass."

While he's talking, he's putting in a pane. He handles it like a baby. He's careful with those screws.

"Every glass you'll ever see sits on two little lead blocks. That divides all the pressure evenly. If it sat flat on the base, it might get a runner, a little crack in the corner, so we always put it on two lead setting blocks.

"And the metal molding is always aluminum. Nothing else is used nowadays.

"Glass is made to bend. A good-sized store window will bend 10 to 12 inches in the wind, if it's not in a bind anywhere. There's a lot of bending, and if it's been put in right, it'll do it every time without breaking.

"Now, most of these glass doors you see are case-hardened glass. Ordinary glass comes in 1-8 inch, 7-32 inch and 1-4 inch thicknesses—case-hardened glass will go right up to one inch thick. You can hit it with a beer bottle, and it won't break. That's because a beer bottle's smooth. But you hit it a lick with something rough, like a rough stone, it will break. It doesn't just break, either, it shatters into a million pieces.

"You know, glass is better than it used to be. We get it out of Libby Owen & Ford in Ohio, and ... "

Who could get excited about glass anyway? Ralph Shoe, that's who. And there are still people who can get excited about laying brick, making chairs and welding metal, too.

So maybe the town cabinet-maker, the one with the pipe in his teeth and the cracker barrel at his side, is gone forever.

He's been replaced.

Throw the learned journals away.

June 1956

Charlie had such a sense of language. And there was just something about his vocal chords—they were operatic.

—Elizabeth Blair Prince,
reporter, *Charlotte News*

From the Pages Of The Old West Strides Determined A.G. Brown

June 1, 1956

WITH HIS FEET PLANTED FIRMLY IN THE DOORWAY OF HIS UNFINISHED BUILDING ON HOSKINS AVE., A.G. Brown resembles a tough Texas rancher in the homesteading days:

"The next blankety-blank building inspector who sets foot on my property without my permission is going to get his head blown off."

Back in the rip-snortin', two-fisted, six-gun West where men were men, a sensible building inspector would have taken the hint and saddled up Old Paint.

But this is the polite, panty-waist, effete East, and this is 1956. They're not listening to that kind of talk in 1956. They're using the Machinery.

The Machinery is nothing but the course of modern justice, but A.G. Brown doesn't know how to cope with it.

"I'm not taking nothing off nobody," Mr. Brown says. "I'll see 'em all in hell first."

Where he'll really see them, of course, is in court on Monday morning, when he must show cause why the restraining order on the construction of his store should not be continued.

"Let 'em try to stop me," he says. "I've got an over-and-under in there that shoots 16 times just as fast as I can pull the trigger. Just let 'em start something."

But nobody wants to shoot it out. All the city wants to do is keep him from building a store in a residential zone.

There are several things about this that Mr. Brown doesn't understand. It's HIS property, isn't it? It's going to be HIS store, isn't it? It isn't even IN the city, is it? So ...

"I'm not taking nothing off nobody."

A.G. Brown figures there's more here than meets the eye, anyway.

"Listen," he says, "you know why Phil Van Every's mad at me?"

He leans in and gives it to you straight, and triumphantly.

"Because when I was a janitor at Alexander Graham Junior High School, I caught him smoking in the cloakroom and took him to the principal, that's why!"

Mr. Brown wanted awfully bad to win the election of the state House last week, partly just so he could walk into Mayor Van Every's office and let him meet the new Representative.

Failing that, he has fallen back on his uncompleted store as the last thing between himself and complete defeat by the city.

"I'm A.G. Brown. I'm 61 years old, and I'm ready to fight," he says.

But when he goes to court Monday, they'll still be fighting him with the Machinery—judges, lawbooks, notarized statements and perimeter zoning regulations. No six-guns.

A.G. Brown was born 100 years too late.

When A Man's 90, Memories Of Boys Grown Old Crowd 'Round

June 4, 1956

Enoch Donaldson has been standing there to greet the graduating class of Davidson College every May since 1883, which is a lot of Mays.

And when Davidson's graduates stepped out into the sunlight from Chambers Auditorium last week with the tassels in their caps swinging in their faces, Enoch Donaldson was there.

Some gave him unknowing looks, and he was sorry about that. He didn't know them.

But he knew their fathers, and their fathers' fathers, and some of these men, old men themselves now, were there to greet him and to inquire about his health after the fashion of old men.

Remarkably little of the education that Enoch Donaldson worked around for so many years ever rubbed off on him. He isn't even sure how old he is, exactly, but thinks he was born three years after "the freedom," which would make him 90.

He can't read and he can't count, but a man doesn't have to know how to count to understand the value of things.

What Enoch Donaldson values is the friendship of the

campus and the town, and he likes to say the names of the old men of Davidson: "Dr. J.B. Shearer," he'll say, "and Dr. Douglas and Dr. Jackson and Dr. Lingle, all friends of mine."

The boys didn't know who it was they were walking by in their moment of pride and accomplishment, but their fathers did, and they walked up to Enoch Donaldson and slapped him on the back.

"Enoch," they'd say, "do you remember the time you were sweeping out my room and a mouse came out ... "

Or, "Enoch," they say, "do you remember the night the train wrecked and spilled liquor all over the tracks ... "

Or, "Remember when President Wilson came to the campus and how the Secret Service tried to keep everybody away ... "

And of course, Enoch was able to summon up all those memories.

The old grads really didn't have to ask.

They should have known that when a man is 90 years old and doesn't have a broom to push or classrooms to keep up or horses to tether on the south campus any more, the memories are what he lives on.

Like a Roofer, Ray Satterfield Covers Domes But He Uses Hair

June 5, 1956

APPEARANCES DECEIVE. Especially if Ray Satterfield has anything to say about it.

Comes the revelation: One out of every 200 Charlotteans is walking around town with a Satterfield toupee on his noggin instead of home-grown hair.

Citizens by the dozens stream into Satterfield's East Blvd. Beauty Shop every month like so many billiard balls.

When they come out, they're blondes, brunettes, redheads, with parts down the middle, left or right—with crewcuts or ducktails—and still without hair on their heads that they can claim for real.

There's more than ideal vanity behind all of this. Take the shiney-headed oil man.

"He came in a couple of years ago," Mr. Satterfield says. "Really unhappy. He had been beaten out of his job by a younger man. So we gave him a hairpiece. The next time I heard from him, he was in South America. Doing very nicely. I got a letter from him the other day. He's in Saudi Arabia. We still send him supplies. He's back in the money again."

Why? Because he has his hair again. Amazing.

"In 15 years," Mr. Satterfield says, "I've had about 2,000 toupee customers. About 1,000 to 1,200 are still on the active list."

Active list?

"Well, you see, a hairpiece wears out in a year to 18 months. Sometimes they break. They last longer if you take them off at night, just like a garment. We don't advise sleeping with them on, though some people do.

"We make them to order right here. They cost $140 to $200 apiece, and women's don't cost any more than men's. All the hair we use is European hair. It's better than American hair because it's bought way up in the mountains, in places where it has never had a permanent wave. It grows tougher that way.

"We can give you any color hair you want, and in style. Wearing a toupee is just like wearing anything else. If you take time to do a good job when you put it on in the morning, it's 92 to 98 percent indetectable. I've seen some even I wouldn't have known for toupees.

"But the idea is not to fool the world anyway. It's the same principle as pads in the shoulders. Everybody knows they're not real, but they make you look better. Same thing with toupees."

Yeah, but think about it. You've got 200 people in your office?

Nobody's bald?

Look closer.

All that glitters is not goldilocks.

Ed Bennett's Dreams
Shaped Like Oranges

June 6, 1956

IF HE HAD STAYED AWAY FROM THE PLANT NURSERY IN FLORIDA, chances are it never would have happened.

But as it was, what could Ed Bennett do?

He visited the nursery with his brother and sister-in-law to see about buying some shrubs and there were the orange trees, dozens of them, barely two feet tall.

It had been a long time since he had seen little ones like that. He thought back 39 years, back to the time he left his father's orange grove between Lakeland and Plant City to make his living elsewhere.

As a Western Union telegrapher, he had been back to Florida many times, he had seen many orange trees, but the little ones with oranges the size of golf balls ...

He found himself reaching into his pocket and paying the man $6.50 for an orange tree. He put it in his car, and he brought it back to Charlotte. He put it in his back yard at 2413 E. 5th St.

It's still small enough to put in the basement on the chilly days. When it gets too large for that, Ed Bennett is going to build a shelter for it next to his garage. He's going to keep the shelter warm with canned heat. He's going to keep that orange tree going.

All the neighbors have come to see it.

"I think they're doubtful about the whole thing," Mr. Bennett admits.

His wife has her doubts too.

"She says I'm making a fool of myself," Mr. Bennett confesses.

But who could agree with a judgment like that? What man doesn't have an orange tree, or some kind of dream tucked in his aspirations?

Climate and temperature at 2413 E. 5th St. do not lend themselves to the cultivation of orange trees. But climate and temperature, you see, have nothing to do with it.

Richard Teesatuskie Discovers Wealth Comes In Many Forms

June 7, 1956

THE WORLD, RICHARD TEESATUSKIE DISCOVERED THIS WEEK, is larger than the Cherokee Indian Reservation.

For the first time in his life, he boarded a bus this week and rode it down out of the mountains. He came to Charlotte, home of Mr. and Mrs. Martin Allen,

who met him last summer when they acted in the Cherokee drama, "Unto These Hills."

He got off the bus into the busiest building he had ever seen, the Charlotte Union Terminal.

("I have two dogs," he said, "and I like to hunt. I have killed squirrel and pheasant with my slingshot.")

He walked down the city streets, gaped at tall buildings, which rise from flat pavement.

He saw rushing traffic, more cars even than the tourists' cars, saw neon lights, watched television for the first time.

("My brother David," he said, "caught a deer last winter. He grabbed it by the horns. We still have the deer's head and feet.")

He went shopping for clothes and shoes in a big department store, he watched a newspaper press roll into high gear, he took his first ride in a ferris wheel.

He saw mighty airplanes landing at a vast field, he stared up at the big dome of the Coliseum. He hardly watched where he was walking, he was so busy looking at something new and astonishing.

("I have 50 strawberry plants," he said. "I won two second places in broad jumping. I know how to hammer silver.")

After two days in Charlotte, Richard Teesatuskie went home to Cherokee. And what did he think after two days, of neon and the buildings and the traffic?

His face was impassive, but his words were clear. "I would not ever want to leave the mountains," he said.

Richard Teesatuskie does not even have a television set. But he has two dogs, 50 strawberry plants, and the head and feet of a deer, which, he noticed, is more than anybody had whom he met in the flat, rushing world beyond the reservation.

Those Red Lights Didn't Exist In The World Of Lucky Walters

June 8, 1956

M OST MEN SPEND THEIR LIVES WAITING FOR THE RED LIGHTS TO CHANGE BEFORE THEY CROSS THE STREET, and that may be why the idea never appealed to Harry Walters.

He came from a normal Union County family, he went to school like the other kids, he played marbles and baseball. When the circus came to town, he went to the circus.

But unlike the other kids, he didn't go home from the circus. He stood there for hour after hour watching the big cats pacing their cages. When the circus train pulled out, Harry Walters was on it.

He didn't know why at the time, and even now, he can't tell you why. But the lions and tigers meant more to him, somehow, than they did to the other youngsters. He worked up to animal trainer.

After that, he joined a touring daredevil show. The cats were fast. But motorcycles and cars were faster, and he learned to drive them as fast as anybody.

While the other kids were going to college, watching the red lights, Harry Walters was doing roll-overs, wing-overs and bus jumps. He was getting shot out of a cannon, walking on airplane wings, leaping through the sky with a parachute on his back.

When he went to Hollywood, it wasn't as an actor. It was as a the guy who jumps off buildings and falls off horses, the guy who gets hit over the head with a chair and plunges through the saloon railing. He took falls for Clark Gable, Audie Murphy, Errol Flynn and Bob Mitchum, and broke bones almost every time.

When he went into the Navy, it wasn't an ordinary job. It was as a detonator extractor and underwater ordinance man.

When he went back to the roadshows, it wasn't as an animal trainer any more. It was as the man who swings on a trapeze 100 feet in the air with no net beneath him. Or as the guy who climbs in a box with eight sticks of dynamite and sets them off.

"Lucky" Walters, the handbills and newspaper stories called him. And Robert ("Believe It or Not") Ripley, impressed by one of Lucky's exploits, called him the world's most amazing stunt man.

That was in 1950, after he caved in his chest, in a bus-jump, got splinted up and took a parachute jump a week later, then drove 426 miles non-stop to another show in which he broke his jaw. As soon as he got out of the hospital, he flipped a midget auto racer and broke his pelvis—and took another parachute jump that night.

Harry Walters came off the circuit this year, settled down to pumping gas at the Spur Station on South Blvd. and keeping an eye on the red lights himself.

He can now. He's proved everything that seemed necessary to be proved when he was watching the lions and tigers that day in Monroe.

Harry Walters went fishing last week for the first time in 18 years.

Mrs. Northam's Lamp Helps Guide Travelers In Trouble

June 11, 1956

T HEY'VE GOT A RIGHT TO MOVE," Mrs. Nan Northam believes.

That goes for anybody.

And when they get lost, or confused, or in trouble, Mrs. Nan Northam, one of the ladies who sits beside a Traveler's Aid lamp in the bus station and in the train terminal, listens.

What do they tell her?

"I guess I'm lost," one old man told her. "I thought I was in Seattle, Washington ... "

"My husband," a pretty teen-aged girl told her, "he was sent to the roads because he stole a tire for our car. I'm hungry and I don't have no place to go until my husband, he comes back ... "

Another girl was about the same age, well-dressed, but determined: "I'm going to New York, and please don't tell my mama where I am ... "

"I can't write, you see," a 72-year-old man told her. "Would you mind ... " And proceeded with as torrid a love letter as Mrs. Nan Northam had ever heard.

And the youngster from a wealthy Asheville family who

had run away with a good-looking boy and married him. He had a yellow convertible and nothing else and he was lying across the motel bed dead drunk.

"I love him," the girl said, "and he will be a great man someday ... if he'll only get a job ... "

"My mother is sick in Newark," a tall, intense man told her. "Don't you believe me?" It took a telephone call to prove he didn't have a mother and had never been to Newark, and another telephone call to get him psychiatric help.

They are blind and crippled, the people who talk to Mrs. Nan Northam. They are alcoholics, runaways, immigrants, children, old folks. They need jobs, tickets, food, beds, sometimes just directions, sometimes just a smile.

They've got a right to move, anybody has.

When they're in trouble, they've got a right to seek help.

When they do, chances are they'll get it from Mrs. Nan Northam.

"I guess I'm lost ... My husband he went to the roads ... Please don't tell my mama ... I can't write ... I love him ... My mother is sick ... "

All in a day's work for the lady beside the lamp.

Be It In Charlotte or Chicago, People Continue To Be People

June 12, 1956

Y OU CAN NEVER GET AWAY FROM BUSINESS, even on vacation, if your business is noticing people and writing about them.

The people are everywhere.

In Hot Springs, N.C., you glance into the face of a bearded man picking wildflowers by the highway. It bears a remarkable resemblance to the bearded face of an Amish citizen walking along Michigan Ave. in Chicago.

The simple calico dress of a blonde girl sitting on a porch near Newport, Tenn., contrasts hardly at all with the simple cotton frock of a blonde girl sitting on her porch in Sheboygan, Wis., and their tresses reflect the same amount of sunlight.

The hotel doormen in Lexington, Ky., and Evanson, Il., make the same remark: "Charlotte, N.C.? That's where Billy Graham's from, ain't it?"

Whenever you get a chance to stop and talk, the people are willing. The publicist of the posh Shore Drive Motel, you find out, used to be a baker.

The soft-spoken owner of Clark Street's famous jazz mecca, the Blue Note, was an iron-worker, then an attendant in a mental hospital, then a railroad man.

The manager of the Sheraton-Blackstone Hotel, where the nation's Democratic Party brass will stay for the Democratic convention in August, is a Vermont farmer's son and was, and is, a Republican.

Sarah Vaughan, the bold singer of songs, is a shy and quiet girl who is scared by audiences.

Rogers Hornsby, the Hall of Fame ballplayer, spends his afternoons nowadays hitting fungoes to the kids in Jackson Park.

You discover things about people whose names you don't know, too:

The farmers along the Wabash and Ohio Rivers, you discover, answer the same disaster in the same way. Both rivers flooded the week before last and drowned the young corn. The farmers went to work last week replanting it—both in Indiana and Ohio.

The people are hard to hold down, just as they are in Charlotte. You pass a trailer with a pine tree limb buckled to it—a shade tree going 55 miles per hour.

You pass a maple tree, a courageous five feet tall, just planted in Chicago's south side slum clearance project, Lake Meadows, and the only tree on the block.

You still do not know, of course, what motivated an iron worker to want to own a jazz emporium, what brought tired old Rogers Hornsby back to the sandlots he started from, what made a resettled Negro decide he must have a maple tree.

But even not knowing these things, you can look into the faces of some of America's people and find justification for repeating an old truth, just for the record:

The good people do not live only on Trade and Tryon Sts. They live also on Wacker Dr. in Chicago and on Main St. in Hurricane, W. Va.

The good people are everywhere.

E.L. Moore Uses Camera, Tricks To Debunk Child-Raising Rules

June 13, 1956

E.L. MOORE IS A CHILD PSYCHOLOGIST WITHOUT PORTFOLIO, couch, notebook, testing apparatus or medical library.

He uses a camera, a feather on a stick and a rubber ball.

He takes pictures of youngsters. He's been doing it in Charlotte, and eloquently, since 1930. Walk into his Little Folks Studio on E. 4th Street and you can find out all about it.

You also might get a few quick tips on child-raising that Dr. Spock never heard of.

To wit:

Suppose the first thing you do is try to win the child's confidence.

"Baloney. I shoot 'em quick, the quicker the better. I never try to win their confidence. I just try to get it over with before they positively dislike me."

Youngsters are pretty hard to get along with, are they?

"Not as hard as their mothers, by and large."

The very young ones are the most difficult to photograph, I suppose.

"Nope. The hardest age is seven or eight years old. They're

self-conscious at that age. The scariest age is two. By that time the kids have made a few trips to the doctor's office, and they figure here we go again."

And you treat them gently to calm them down?

"Oh no. I bop myself on the head with the bulb and make silly faces. Only way to handle the scary ones."

Having been in business here for so long, I guess you know a lot of people, don't you?

"You'd be surprised at how many folks come in here with their babies and tell me, 'You made my picture when I was a baby. Remember? Remember?' How could I? They've changed."

Do you ever take pictures of adults, by the way?

"Reluctantly. Women always try to look 29. When they get a certain age, they shouldn't have their pictures made. The kids aren't worried about looking as old as they really are."

You sound, sir, a little cynical about the whole thing.

"Not at all. I love to take pictures of youngsters. It honestly still gives me a kick.

"I don't know what I'd do without the little devils."

Trash Dump 'Prospector' Finds Every Silver Lining Has Cloud

June 14, 1956

T HE OLD ROCK QUARRY ON TREMONT AVE. was never anything but a pain in the neck, anyway, always catching fire, sending firemen out to spend the taxpayers' money ...

So they issued an order: No more dumping junk and paper.

That suited everybody.

Everybody but Will James.

For years, Will James has had the concession at the rock hole. He sits there in a rocking chair and keeps people from dumping their trash in the street.

In return for that, he gets to sort through each load of trash and keep whatever of value he can find.

It used to be a pretty good deal. Load after load would come in and Will James would be kept busy tramping over the pile, looking for things to sell.

He'd find plenty of paper and he'd stack it up and call the man to come get it. That was always good for a dollar or two.

Or he'd find auto springs and radiators. Once or twice, he found a watch. Every now and then, he'd even find money, "nothing bigger than a quarter or fifty cents," but there was always the chance ...

Now, there isn't even a chance.

"They don't dump nothing here but brickbats and mortar," he said.

He bit on a piece of watermelon he had brought along to keep him company, and he spat out the seeds one by one, thoughtfully.

"Every once in a long while, somebody will dump a load of something I can get a dollar or two out of. So I just stay on. A man has to do something ... "

It was three o'clock in the afternoon, and the sun was "high and hot."

"There ain't a single load been brought here today," Will James said. "It's all going to the land fill off Statesville Ave. now."

He motioned out to the piles of dirt with his watermelon knife.

"There's hundreds of dollars worth of stuff buried out there," he said. "I didn't have time to get it. Now I have plenty of time, and I can't get it.

"All this stuff on top of the dirt ain't worth a dime."

One of these days, the fill will be completed, the bulldozers will level off the dirt over the Tremont Ave. rock hole, and they'll put up a sign: "No Dumping."

"I'll leave then," Will James said.

Every silver lining has a cloud.

Cecil Brodt's Life
Filled With Sounds

June 15, 1956

I T ALL STARTED WHEN CECIL BRODT DID A FAVOR FOR A FRIEND.

"He was thinking about buying a speaker for his record player," he remembers, "and I went along to help him size it up."

He listened to the tones coming out of the speaker cabinet, the richness, the quality, the highs, the lows, the sheer glory of it all—and became an audiophile on the spot.

Even before that, Cecil Brodt, owner of Brodt Music Co., had a pretty good acquaintance with sound, as musician and music salesman.

"But that was really an experience," he says. "The guy put 'Anitra's Dance' by Grieg on that turntable, and for the first time in my life, I heard an oboe on a record sound like an oboe."

What has happened since is measured in revolutions per minutes and cycles per second. Cecil Brodt has become the town's best known hi-fi exponent. He sells 'em, he installs 'em, he even makes 'em.

"See that cabinet in the corner?" he asks. "Our own make. We had the Celanese Audio Club out here and we tried a few cabinets on them, matching professional cabinets against our own.

"Seventy percent of them liked ours best.

"The secret is in the slanted front. We discovered that accidentally when we were installing a system at the Barringer Hotel. We had to slant the speakers to make them fit up under the ceiling.

"Wonderful sound! You discover things in crazy ways."

Before you can say him nay, he'll dash to a nearby tape machine and put on a tape. A direct recording of the Pee Wee Russell, Wild Bill Davidson & Co. and something out of Storyville. He'll turn it way up high.

"Listen to that Wild Bill," he'll say. "Listen to that high note.

"I play a little horn myself, you know.

"And listen to that cabinet. No vibration.

"Listen to that speaker. When you turn it up, no blasting. It just gets louder.

"Will you listen to that Wild Bill!"

If you listen, you'll have to admit it sounds just fine.

And how much does it cost?

"For a really fine system? Let's see ... $165 for a good speaker, $80 for that cabinet, $129 for an amplifier, $37.50 for a cartridge, $54.50 for a turntable, $5 for a base for the turntable. Add it up ... $462.

"But a high fidelity system that is perfectly satisfactory can be assembled for under $200. All depends on such things as the size of your tweeters and woofers."

Not being nosy—and not having a handy $462—you don't ask about tweeters and woofers.

But there's one question you would like answered. What happened to that speaker that was so good on the "Anitra's Dance" oboe? Did the friend buy it?

"Nope," says Cecil Brodt. "I bought it."

C.R. Zachary Finds Ice Nice, But It's Gone Modern On Him

June 18, 1956

T HE ICEMAN STILL COMETH.

But he doesn't come with a block of ice hanging miraculously between the tips of a pair of tongs. Not any more.

He doesn't come to the back porch, open the screen door and slide his ice cold burden into the icebox with the shout of, "ICEman!"

All that is gone, though C.R. Zachary, manager of Electric Ice & Fuel Co., can remember when putting ice in iceboxes was 95 percent of his company's business.

And the colored cards people used to hang on their front doors, black meaning "no ice today, thanks," and red meaning, "ice, please"?

"Haven't seen one in years," C.R. Zachary says. "I doubt if there are 50 home iceboxes in Charlotte today. If there are, the people buy it here at the loading dock. We don't have any home deliveries any more. But we're selling more ice than ever before, upwards of 50 tons a day.

"I don't know—maybe that means that people are drinking more liquor. Of course, it means that people are drinking more cold beverages than ever before. There's a big demand for sized ice, snow, nut and egg-sized. We sell huge truckloads of it to restaurants and packing houses, places like that. But we have 26 little ice stations in the county and they sell it like crazy."

All around, there are huge engines pumping away. Beneath the floor, brine is circulating among 288 cans full of water.

"It takes 60 hours for each of these cans to produce 300 pounds of ice," C.R. Zachary says. "The ice is moved mechanically into the storage room. Then we can sell it in blocks, crushed or sized. Machines do most of the work. We also make ice punchbowls and swans and things in a mold and I then I polish them up by hand. We even freeze roses into the punchbowl."

Roses. There's one to paste into your hat. Especially if you are one of those romantics who think nothing has changed in this supersonic world.

Note, please, the passing of the "ICEman!" shout, the coming of "snow" and "eggs," of 26 stations and giant pumps, of trucks and heavy machinery to this quietest and quaintest of industries.

The iceman still cometh. With roses.

B.L. Kasselik Mourns Passing Of True Art

June 19, 1956

W HEN B.L. KASSELIK ENTERED THE ROYAL ACADEMY in Budapest 40 years ago, people cared something about art.

When they built a fine house, they wanted it decorated. They wanted a stately, beautiful design and they wanted a few acanthus leaves on a Corinthian column, and maybe an entrance door in the fashion of the Italian Renaissance.

"Nowadays," B.L. Kasselik says bitterly, "beauty is a nonexistent something. Houses are made of glass and steel and God knows what. It is a plumber who makes the design."

And then (in the glory days) after the house was built, they wanted it filled with art. A few paintings, a bust or a statue.

"Who wants a statue now?" B.L. Kasselik asks. "I couldn't give one away!"

B.L. Kasselik can look around from his studio on Old Pineville Rd. and see that the things he thinks are beautiful are fighting a rear guard action against modern art.

"Once I met a modern artist," he says. "It was in New York. He told me had bought a canvas and a frame and he was going to paint a picture.

"He had even figured out what he was going to called it: 'The Unicorn'

"He knew a unicorn looked like a horse, but he didn't know how to draw a horse. So I sketched him a few horses and he went to work.

"He won first prize in an exhibit.

"That's modern art!"

B.L. Kasselik figured out long ago that the South, with its more conservative tastes in art, is the place for him. Except for a few years during the war, he's been in Charlotte since 1926.

He stays busy. Right now, he's working on the intricate, detailed interior of the Tryon Palace restoration, soon to open in New Bern. He's making a huge U.S. Marine emblem to decorate the Marine training center. He's constructing mantels and cornices.

He'd like to do a bust or a figure again, as artists have done since thousands of years before Christ. But there's no demand for busts or figures "unless they look like eggs balanced on top of one another."

What does an artist do in a time when beauty as he knows it is a non-existent something?

"I do whatever I can," B.L. Kasselik says. "My mantels and cornices and emblems."

And his art?

"I try not to think about it."

The Governor's No Caruso, But He's Proud Of His Vocal Chords

June 20, 1956

Every man has something he's proud of. With the Governor, it's his lungs.

He's got a larynx like a desert horn and a 13-year-old song that goes: "HEY, getcha *Charlotte News* final eDITion PAPer today here!"

If you've passed Thacker's in the middle of the day, you know the Governor. If you happen to be a pretty girl, you're likely to know him very well.

With the men, the Governor plays it dignified: "Paper today, sir!"

The girls get softened up: "You look like you've been down to Myrtle Beach, honey pie."

"Thank you," one answers.

"You're welcome as the flowers in June," the Governor says. "Paper?"

The Governor's name is Eugene Broughton, no relation to the late J. Melville, and he's been selling the *News* in front of Thacker's ever since he left the farm at Garner to see the bright lights.

He begins at 11 a.m. when the first edition is off the press—"I'm the first man to Tryon St. with those papers. Boy, I trot right along"—and he doesn't quit until eight o'clock, with the pink final down at the bus station.

He wears an ancient felt hat and keeps his Adam's apple hopping. You can't sell papers sitting down, boy, and you can't sell papers without talking it up."

He yanks his papers out of the stack under his arm with a pop.

"You got to show some enthusiasm, boy. I sell about 290 a day. When there's a murder, I sell maybe 320. I started out hollering right from the beginning, and the only day I ever had a sore throat was the second day, way back during the war."

The Governor is essentially a modest guy.

"I don't like to brag," he says. "But I really do believe I can outholler most people."

He takes you by the arm.

"See how far it is from here to the Liberty Life Building?" he asks.

It's pretty far.

"Well, one time a fellow who works at that radio station up there told me he was standing at the window and he heard me way down here and he could hear what I was saying."

Every man has something he's proud of.

With the Governor, that's it.

With Backyard As Stage, John Gives Concert For Youngsters

June 21, 1956

Y OU COULD HEAR THE MUSIC WAY UP ON MOREHEAD ST.

It was coming from an amplified guitar in the hands of a man standing in a Vance St. back yard.

He had a big crowd around him, mostly young-sters. There was a woman washing clothes on the porch, and two men leaning against a house tapping time with their toes, and one old  man sitting in his second-floor window, reading a newspaper and listening.

But the rest were boys and girls, standing in a big semi-circle. One boy, six or seven years old, sat on the guitar loud-speaker, feeling the vibrations and grinning.

The guitar player was John Honeycutt. His music drifted through the rows of houses and the crowd got bigger.

"It's like this every time I play," he said. "I just do it for the kids around here."

John Honeycutt has a four-piece band. Tuesday nights, he plays at the Zanzibar, Thursday nights at the Vet's Club, weekends he plays for dances and parties.

In the afternoon, he plays for the kids.

"The way it happened," he said, "some of 'em started pestering me to play for 'em one day. They hadn't ever heard any music except on the radio and records. I wasn't doing anything else, so I figured I might as well."

John Honeycutt had never heard music, either, when he was growing up. He had learned how to play the guitar from a 50-cent book. He bought the book before he bought the guitar.

"I would have given anything to have somebody play me music. You know how it is," he said. "It's nothing much."

That's right, it's nothing much.

To anybody but the kids.

After One Year and Two Days, Dreams Were Clouded By Tears

June 22, 1956

IT TOOK MRS. ETHEL SLOOP EXACTLY ONE YEAR and two days to break down and cry. For one year and two days, nothing could disappoint her. The size of her dream eclipsed the odds against it ever coming true.

Her dream was a job for every Mecklenburg man or woman who wanted one.

Last week, for the first time, she saw the odds clearly.

She was a bookkeeper who lost her job last year because she was "too old." Wherever she went to apply for another job, she got the same answer: "We don't hire anyone over 40."

Mrs. Ethel Sloop just didn't happen to believe that life ends at 40. So she took the last two words of that phrase and made it the war cry of the "Over 40 Club."

She stopped looking for a job herself and became a one-woman employment agency. Her service was free. The only requirement for membership: You must be over 40, and out of a job.

She began pestering newspapers and the employment agency and business executives—anyone who would listen.

She wrote letters to the mayor, the governor, the senators and representatives from North Carolina.

She went without sleep, without food. The size of her effort, in retrospect, seems fantastic.

Everywhere, she met resistance. Employment people reminded her they had been trying to provide jobs for older workers for years with only limited success. Businessmen argued that older workers run up the group insurance rates. The United Appeal turned down her appeal for funds.

Mrs. Sloop just tossed her red curls and flung statistics back in their faces. Studies show that older workers are better workers. They deserve a chance. She preached her sermon a thousand times. She deluged them with literature.

Membership in her club grew from 100 to 200 to 300. She found jobs personally for nearly half of them. She prodded the rest to pound the pavement for themselves.

"These people think they're at the end of the road," she said. "They don't know what to do. I tell them what to do—fight!"

Mrs. Ethel Sloop fought. She set up an office in a church hut at 705 N. Pine St. Without money or help, she stayed there every day, all day long, talking on the phone, looking for jobs.

Last week, two days after the club's first anniversary, Mrs. Sloop planned a big dinner. She invited 150 people—active club members, executive board members, businessmen.

She ordered the food and spread the table.

Thirty showed up.

Mrs. Ethel Sloop looked at the 120 empty places and felt the sudden, heavy hand of despair for the first time in one year and two days.

The walls of her dream fell in.

Now, a week later, she's building them back again. She is going on television Monday at one o'clock with a collection of businessmen and public officials on her side.

She cried for only five minutes, which, even for an uncommon woman like the redhead of Pine St., is not above par for the course.

Rush Operation To Aid Lundy, And It Will Help Anita, Too

June 25, 1956

T HIS IS MARGARET COBLE'S STORY, and it is true except for the names, and it starts with a broken doll.

The doll is sitting on a shelf at Mrs. Coble's Doll Hospital on South Blvd., its cracked plastic head hanging crazily to one side, its arms limp.

"This one belongs to Anita," Mrs. Coble said. "Its name is Lundy. It's a rush job."

Anita is five years old and Lundy, the doll, is almost that old. Anita has had Lundy with her ever since she can remember. Lundy went to bed with her at night and woke up with her in the morning, and whenever Anita went anywhere, Lundy went too.

"When Anita got sick last year," Mrs. Coble said, "Lundy went to the hospital with her for a few days. She went to kindergarten right along with Anita."

Last month, Anita's dad died. The little girl, her mother and two brothers, moved from their house to an apartment.

In the course of moving, Anita's doll was knocked from a cabinet to the floor and broken. Anita, who didn't understand everything that was happening, put Lundy in her doll bed and said nothing about it.

Anita's mother, sick and unable to work, decided two weeks ago that Anita and her brothers would have to go into a children's home until she was able to care for them again.

She explained that to Anita, very carefully. Everything would be all right, she said, and Anita agreed.

But the little girl had a question she wanted to ask. She didn't know whether she should, but she finally burst out: What about Lundy?

So last week, Lundy came to the Doll Hospital, to Mrs. Margaret Coble, and Anita's mother told Mrs. Coble the story. Lundy, she said, had to be ready by Wednesday.

"It's a rush job," Mrs. Coble said. "And it's free, of course."

Wherever Anita goes, Lundy goes.

Room Full Of Clocks Ticks Out New Life For Query Alexander

June 26, 1956

P UTTING NEW WORKS INTO A CLOCK," Query Alexander said, "is almost like putting new life into a man."

Which is exactly what happened to Query Alexander.

After a heart attack three years ago, he was laid up for four months with nothing to do.

A couple of clocks around the house needed fixing. He had never taken a clock apart before in his life, but he took these apart, and he got them running.

The ticking of those two clocks started a new life for Query Alexander.

A neighbor, trying to fix a clock of his own, failed miserably. "The mainspring bounced out of there and flew all over creation," Query Alexander said.

So the neighbor brought his clock over, and Query Alexander , with more patience than he had ever been willing to use before, put it back together again.

When the doctors finally let him out of bed, Query Alexander bought a couple of clocks from a junk dealer, and he bought a couple of books about clocks.

He looked his new clocks up in the book and he discovered that one was fairly valuable, worth more than he had paid for it.

When he had fixed those clocks—made a new case for one of them, a new gear for another, replaced the pictures on the front and cleaned the faces—he bought another clock.

He found that down in his workshop, he forgot his heart attack and the painful months in bed.

Every tick of the clocks above his workbench brought him nearer recovery, and every time he finished one clock and put it on the shelf to tick beside the other, he bought another one.

He searched for clocks in all stages of disrepair. Each was a new thrill.

He found clocks with wooden gears, clocks with faces that move and hands that stand still. He found "roosterhead," "beehive," "steeple," and wall clocks. He found "corset" clocks and "acorn" clocks, metal clocks and china clocks.

He took a lot of time with them, bringing them back to the condition they were in when other craftsmen made them and sold them years ago.

Query Alexander, once a vigorous deputy sheriff and once an energetic operator of a merchant's protective association, is now a quiet collector of clocks.

"I'm just as sure as I can be that these clocks have kept me alive," he said.

Have you ever heard 73 clocks strike four o'clock all at once? It is a fine sound.

Cincinnati-To-Charlotte Road, Full Of Music For Miss Lolly

June 27, 1956

T HE NAME IS LOLLY HOWARD.

She's a grandmother now, but she's got a bouncy tune in her heart.

"And if you'd care to hear that 'Swanee River' played in ragtime ... "

... Miss Lolly is your gal.

She started out playing an organ at the Keith's circuit theater in Cincinnati, and she ended up a couple of weeks ago in Charlotte with a basket of flowers—"a great big thing like a Hollywood person would get"—given to her by her piano students.

In between ...

Well, in between it was wonderful.

There were the house-to-house music lessons for 50 cents a throw in the old days in Charlotte.

There was the band, "Lolly Howard's Carolina Swingsters," and the tours all through the South in the golden days of band music, the 30s; the one-nighters with Pete, the drummer, and Marco, the sax man, for seven years.

There were club dates and dance dates and always, always

the happy sound of a driving trumpet and bouncing bass.

There were the early days on WBT with a guy named "Wayside Brown" and Miss Lolly's theme song: "Dear one, the world is waiting for the sunshine … "

From playing a hot organ for Irene Dunne, cats, acrobats, dance teams and comedians at Keith's … to playing piano for Jim Farley and Clyde R. Hoey … to a wonderful night a long time ago at the Southern Railroad Station, and a jam session beside the tracks with Tommy Dorsey … to that recital and all the flowers, and a man who flew all the way from Washington just to hear Miss Lolly swing into "Alexander's Ragtime Band" …

To the day when the doctors told her 40 years of swinging it was enough. No more shows …

From beginning to end, "I've had a wonderful, wonderful, wonderful time."

"There no business like show business … "

And nobody in it quite like Miss Lolly.

Baseball's Golden Days Received Added Sparkle From 'Hello' Bill

June 28, 1956

A WORD TO THE FRIENDS OF BILL STARR:

His name's not Bill.

It's Ernest A.—but "that's just between us."

Nobody's called him Ernest since 1915, when he took a megaphone with "El-Rees-So Cigars" written on it and started walking around the streets of Charlotte whomping up attendance for the Hornet baseball games.

Bill Starr remembers the words of his chant exactly.

It went, "Hello, Bill, you going to the ball game? I'll see you! I'll be there!"

He's been "Hello" Bill Starr ever since—through years of working for the City Water Department and almost as many years selling tickets at Griffith Park.

Where the Hornets went, Bill Starr and his megaphone went—to Winston-Salem, Greensboro, Durham—with "Hello, Bill, going to the ball game?"

He didn't help the Hornets much.

"In 1915," he says, "they lost their first 11 games, won the 12th and lost 13 more.

"But then we swapped managers with Augusta. Burleigh

Emory went down there and we got Martin Dudley. Dudley brought a bunch of south Georgia boys up here, and we won the pennant in 1916."

They were Golden Days for baseball.

"I remember Chief Bender. He was pitching semi-pro ball for Gastonia and Jap Efird was pitching for Red Springs, and they had a big series out at Wearn Field—later, it was Hayman Park—and over on Mint Street.

"Bender was really something. Funniest thing I ever saw was one time when he laid a bunt down the first base line, then trotted along on top of it so nobody could get to it—and the runner on third scored that way, you see ... "

Bill Starr is retiring tomorrow from the Water Dept.

He'll clean the things out of his desk, and he'll go home. There'll be plenty of time for watching ball games this summer.

One of the things he'll take with him when he goes is a paper weight bearing a picture of a young man with a megaphone. It was given to him in 1915. It says, "Hello, Bill."

Nobody calls him Ernest.

With Lump In Throat, Gus Plans For Future

June 29, 1956

IF LOSING THE SOAP BOX DERBY SOUNDS LIKE ONLY A MINOR LEAGUE TRAGEDY TO YOU, that just shows how old you are.

There's only one winner, and it wasn't Gustevas Roberts.

Gus was the last Charlotte boy eliminated.

He won his first heat and his second heat, and that put him into the quarterfinals, and he won that, too.

Then, with only four boys left in his class, and only two races away from the gold trophy and the trip to Akron, Gus Roberts lost.

A dozen other boys crowded around him before his car stopped, and they said, "Don't feel bad, Gus," and "You did fine, Gus," the way boys seek awkwardly to comfort one another.

Gustevas Roberts climbed out of his car and watched while they loaded Tony Osbon's racer on to a truck for the trip back to the top of the raceway and the championship hat.

A few minutes later, he stood on the edge of the crowd and watched Val Hawkins, the champion, being interviewed on the radio.

"I tried real hard," he said. "The other boy's wheels were

broken in better. I worked on mine for three months, but he worked on his for four months."

They were a busy three months, with advice from his mother, and from Dr. Russell, a dentist in his Brevard St. neighborhood, and from his buddy, Isiah.

They were a three months spent on balancing and laminating and polishing, and hoping. And they ended up with Gustevas Roberts on the edge of the crowd.

"My first year, I lost in my first heat and last year I lost in my second heat," Gus Roberts said.

He looked over at his car, the one he spent three months on.

"I've got one more year," he said. "I'm going to build another one. It's going to be better."

There was a lump in his throat.

"I'm going to start tomorrow," he said.

July 1956

He wrote about people's troubles and triumphs. There was nothing of what used to be called the sob sister element in his writing. If somebody was having a bad time, his writing reflected that. But it was not "bringing out the crying towel" by any means. There was an absence of anything that was unnecessary. His writing was clean and cut right to the point, and yet it reflected his own personality in a way that wasn't really obvious.

—Bud Cox,
book editor, *Charlotte News*

Ice Cream King Is Proud Champ; He'll Take On All Challenges

July 2, 1956

IN THIS CORNER, wearing the pistachio trunks with the chocolate ripple stripe, weighing 190 pounds, the Ice Cream Eating Champion of the Carolinas, Rembert Garris.

Mr. Garris, director of the YMCA Fresh Air Camp on the Catawba, came by his title in the only honest way, beating the former champion.

And if there's anybody in the audience who thinks he can best Mr. Garris in the free-style ice cream eating, why let him load his butter pecan in his car and motor on out. Rembert Garris is a fighting champ.

In a way, Rembert Garris' story is the story of America. There was a time when he was just another hard-working YMCA official, anonymous, unrecognized.

Then, in half an hour, there he was, on top of the ice cream eating heap.

The record, before he came along, was 28 large scoops consumed in 30 minutes. It was held by the general secretary of the Spartanburg, S.C., YMCA, a gentleman foolhardy enough to accept Mr. Garris' challenge.

The two went to an ice cream parlor. They were accompanied by managers—"to make sure," Mr. Garris says, "that everybody got a fair scoop."

They squared off with soup bowls and, at a signal, began eating.

His opponent picked vanilla. Mr. Garris, confident almost to the point of cockiness, expansive, flamboyant, ordered vanilla, chocolate, strawberry, peach, pistachio, butter pecan and peppermint.

Scoop followed scoop. After 15 minutes, the two had put away 17 scoops apiece. Mr. Garris poured on the coal. After 20 minutes, the score was 25-21, Mr. Garris leading.

After 30 scoops, the Spartanburg pretender was vanquished. Rembert Garris had 36 scoops under his belt when the half-hour was over.

They're calling him "36-scoop" Garris now. He's the champ, the idol of ice cream eaters from Due West to Mt. Airy.

His prize, naturally, was a quart of ice cream.

And what did he do with it?

"I," said Rembert Garris in the fashion of the true competitor he is, "ate it."

C.C. Leonard Turned 'Tiring' Nightmares Into Business

July 3, 1956

BEFORE WORLD WAR II, C.C. Leonard was in the milk business in Raleigh, so when he went into the Army, naturally he was put to operating the largest tire recapping station in the world.

"Sooner or later," he remembers, "every truck tire in the Third and Ninth Armies came through there."

"We'd have 250,00 tires piled up at one time.

"You've never seen so many tires. NOBODY had ever seen so many tires.

"We'd recap 1,200 tires every 12 hours, working right around the clock, and never make a dent in all those tires."

Most people's nightmares involve three-headed monsters. C.C. Leonard's were full of tire machines and tire tracks.

Brussels was a long way from Raleigh, and there was a big difference between the calm, benevolent milk business and millions of tires, and there were days when C.C. Leonard would walk around and look at all those tires and dream about the time he could get back in civilian clothes and never look at a tire again.

That day came.

He got back into civilian clothes.

He left all those tires behind.

And on his way across the Atlantic, he discovered something:

He missed the tires.

Meet C.C. Leonard, president of the Shaw Royal Tire Co., dealer in auto tires, truck tires, tractor tires and road grader tires, and specialist in recapping—

Tires.

With Courtroom As Classroom, Lt. White Forms A New Alphabet

July 4, 1956

L T. ALLEN WHITE'S DAILY ALPHABET is different from the one he learned in grammar school.

("A" is for assault. "B" is for burglary. "C" is for Carrying Concealed Weapon.)

"Now, Lootenant," the big guy said with a go in, "I was just toting that 45 over to my friend's house. You know I wouldn't do nobody no harm ... "

Lt. Allen White, clerk of the City's Recorder's Court, is a patient man. He has heard it all before.

("D" is for Disorderly Conduct. "E" is for Embezzlement. "F" if for Forgery.)

"Forgery is a mighty bad word," the fat woman with the gold tooth said. "I was just trying to get me a little money to buy some groceries. You know a body's got to eat, Lootenant."

Lt. Allen White is celebrating, if that is the word, 15 years in the City Police Dept. this week. For 13 of those years, he's been opening and closing court, swearing in witnesses, and listening.

("G" is for Gambling. "H" is for Habitual Drunkenness.)

"If I can get off this time, Lootenant, I'll never be back again," the old man said. "I was on my way to the bus station when the officer picked me up. I was heading to the Veteran's Home in Mountain Home, Tennessee, and I had just had two beers as a sort of goodbye to Charlotte ... "

He's heard it from Paregoric Annie, who drinks paregoric; from Horseface, who drinks liquor; from Chicken John, who carefully avoids drinking anything, but who steals chickens; and from a hundred thousand other citizens with less colorful names but with no less inclination toward getting themselves arrested.

"And do you know what?" Lt. Allen White said, upon passing his 15th year on the force. "Most of the people I come across are pretty doggone decent. Sometimes I want to get a stick after them ... but I haven't soured on the human race, not one bit."

("L" is for Larceny, "M" is for Manslaughter, "N" is for Narcotics.)

"I try to trust them all as much as they'll let me," Lt. Allen White said. "I'm responsible for the fines, and I've let hundreds of them go home to get money. The only one who ever tried to beat me out of anything was a boy from a nice neighborhood and a good family ...

"You can't ever tell about people."

("O" is for Operating Auto Under Influence. "P" is for prostitution.)

After 15 years, Lt. Allen White is still, somehow, full of the human virtues, and nobody in this town can beat him for patience and warmth of spirit.

Even though "A," in his corner of the city, is not for Apple.

City's Squirrel Expert Keeps City Hall Lawn Charges Happy

July 5, 1956

T HIS IS JOE MELTON, leaning against the City Hall wall, looking out at the lawn with the shadow of big oaks spread out on it and talking:

"I feed the squirrels. Peanuts that fall on the floor over at Swinson Food Products. They sweep 'em up and sell 'em to us, and I feed 'em to the squirrels every afternoon at 4:30.

"We've got 26. We had 28, but two of 'em got run over crossing the street.

"That's one thing about squirrels. When they decide they want to leave, they leave. Some of them go miles out in the country. Those two just didn't make it."

Joe Melton shifts his feet and uses his shoulder to lean with.

"We've got one brown squirrel. That really is something. I never saw one like him and George Livingston (the city accountant) says he never saw one like him, either.

"A brown squirrel is something like a white crow. You get one every million or so. Most squirrels look a little brown on the back, but they're really gray. This one is brown all over.

"I've been feeding squirrels for about seven years. Dick

Basinger used to do it, but he quit fooling with them.

"They hardly ever come all at once. On a wet day, when the sun comes out, they'll all come down from the trees, but that's the only time."

While he talks, a squirrel jumps up on the bird bath and sips at the water, poking his head up and looking around every couple of seconds.

"Cats and dogs are hard on these squirrels. The young ones are here now and they live in mortal fear of cats. One thing: A squirrel can beat a cat up a tree. That's lucky.

"A cat will get so far up a tree and he'll realize he'd better go back down. Squirrels and coons are the only things that'll come down a tree head foremost. Squirrels have forgotten more about climbing trees that cats will ever learn."

In the big building behind him, Henry A. Yancey is running the city's government, George Livingston is keeping the books, Herman Hoose is worrying about traffic problems.

Only Joe Melton gets to lean against the wall and watch the gray shadows on the big lawn and talk about the squirrels.

The Tired Milkman Was Wrong; It Wasn't 'Just Another Day'

July 6, 1956

T HE MILKMAN, WHO NEEDED A SHAVE, finished his coffee and yawned.

He turned around on his stool and looked out at gray, empty E. 4th St. for a minute, and then he turned back to the counter and said, "I guess I'll have another cup of coffee, Ken," and then he yawned again.

"Just another day, boy," he said. "One of these days, I'm going to stop going to work at 4 o'clock in the morning and start getting me some sleep."

Kenneth Stavrakas, who goes to work at Ringside Grill at eight o'clock at night, handed him his coffee and leaned against the back side of the counter with his arms folded.

The milkman blew the steam from his coffee and sipped it cautiously.

"It was raining when I got up," he said. "You get any rain?"

"Just a little," Kenneth Stavrakas said, "about midnight."

The sun came from behind a cloud and it got brighter outside.

Nobody said anything until the milkman finished his coffee, stretched, and walked over to the door, leaving a couple of dimes behind.

He stood there aimlessly before he left. "Another day," he said. "Guess, I'll got get some sleep."

"Goodbye," Ken said. He cleared away the coffee cup. On his way back to the kitchen, he noticed the calendar.

It said, "Tuesday, July 3." Kenneth Stavrakas pulled that leaf off, and then it said, "Wednesday, July 4."

"Hey," he said, "I got something to do here."

He went back into the storeroom and rummaged around for a minute, and came out with a big American flag already hooked to a pole.

While he was unwinding it, he said, "I got to go home and help my boy put his flag up, too. He's only four, but he's crazy about that flag. He wants to get it out there."

Kenneth Stavrakas walked out the front door. He stuck the pole into a socket in the sidewalk. The sun was behind a cloud again. The flag moved slightly in a little breeze.

"Just another day," the milkman called it.

He forgot, that's all.

Being Topsy-Turvy Not New
Sensation to John

July 9, 1956

Y OU'D THINK JOHN CLIFFORD, an upright 17-year-old, would have something better to do than go around hanging by his heels over city streets wearing a straitjacket.

But that's where he was two years ago—when he was just 15—in Columbia, S.C., and that's where he'll be again this summer in Greensboro.

John Clifford is training to take up where Houdini left off. Or if not that, to settle down into some equally colorful niche of show business. Hanging upside down from fire truck ladders is just part of the game.

He's got a basement full of tricks, a dog named "Prestidigitation" and a patient father, James H. Clifford.

"My dad held me from a tree limb with a rope while I practiced my straitjacket trick," John says. "And then I stood on my head a little to get the feel of it."

Having gotten the feel of it, he wowed the Southeastern Magicians Association by escaping from the jacket in four minutes.

John learned the secret by spending a day with Houdini's book collection in the rare books rooms of the Library of

Congress in Washington.

At first, because of his age, they wouldn't let him in. So he walked over to the Senate Office Building, did a trick for Sen. Willis Smith, and got the doors opened.

He got his eyes opened, too. "Houdini was a great, versatile man," he says. "There's never been another like him."

John, the youngest member ever admitted to the International Brotherhood of Magicians, took up hypnotism a couple of years ago.

"At first, I just hypnotized my relatives. But then Bridey Murphy came along, and everybody got interested in it. I've averaged one a day since then."

And what does he think of Bridey?

"Phony as a three-dollar-bill," he says. "It sets back the search for truth about extra-sensory perception."

John Clifford's private search is for new fields to conquer. At 17, he's come near exhausting the standard magic repertoire.

He has an eye on radio-TV, or acting, or some other branch of show business.

It can be straight and narrow—but he'd prefer that it be right side up.

Chief Brown Employs Phonetics To Decide On Final Assignment

July 10, 1956

So HERE WAS CHIEF PETTY OFFICER FRANK BROWN, sitting in San Diego, Calif., where he owns not one but two houses, soaking up the sun, with 28 years of Navy Service behind him, and two more years to go for retirement at the age of 44, and the Navy was urging him to spend those two years right there in San Diego, or in Hawaii, if he'd like to.

And so what did he do?

He reached up on the shelf sort of lazily, and he took down the atlas.

There was Monroe, La., where he enlisted in 1928 after getting tired of hoeing in the field.

There was Cuba, Haiti, Panama, where he was first stationed.

Chief Frank Brown let his eye roam over the atlas, and he thought about those palm-fringed ports and those ocean breezes, and he let his eye keep roaming, and it stopped on Charlotte, N.C.

"Wonder," he said to his wife, "what Charlotte, N.C., is like?"

"We know what Hawaii is like," she said.

"Uh-huh," Chief Frank Brown said. "I think I'll write to the Chamber of Commerce back there and just see."

The literature told him Charlotte, N.C., was the Queen City of the South and it had lots of churches and plenty of nice places to live.

"I think ... " Chief Frank Brown said.

"Frank ... " his wife said.

" ... we'll try Charlotte, N.C.," Chief Frank Brown said.

No reason, you understand, except that Chief Frank Brown is a man who likes new places, and he liked the way "Charlotte, North Carolina" rolled off the tongue, and he liked that "Queen City" business.

Chief Frank Brown is over at the recruiting station in the Post Office, his wife is working for a doctor.

"We had some of the neighbors over for a Navy movie the other night," Chief Frank Brown said.

"Wonderful people.

"Wonderful town."

Busy Izzie Deals Pasteboards For Charlotte's Entertainment

July 11, 1956

T HE GUY OUTSIDE THE NATIONAL HAT SHOP HAD IT RIGHT.

"Izzie?" he said. "Izzie's an institution, man."

And so he is, man, a real, solid gold, long suffering, 100 percent institution right on Independence Square.

Solid gold, because that's what he's worth his weight in to promoters like Jim Crockett, for who Izzie Silverstein sells tickets at a counter in the hat shop and in the sundry box offices of the city.

Mr. Crockett, a superstitious gentleman who doesn't like to think about money until two or three days after the paying customers have been charmed by Little Richard or Gorgeous George and the taxes have all been paid, leaves the money up to Izzie.

Then he comes into the shop as if how things went is the last thing on earth that could concern him, raises an eyebrow at Izzie Silverstein and gets the word.

This is Izzie's 26th year as Charlotte's ticket king. He took over from one Joe Miller at Hunter-House Cigar Store, Church and Trade Sts., in 1930.

If there are a few silver threads among the gold today, you

must realize that the life of a ticket seller is not all a matter of knowing how to make change.

"For instance," says Izzie, "the kid at the rock and roller last week. I had my eye on him. He got in on a $1.50 ticket and he was standing around a locked door. All of a sudden, sure enough, he unlocked it. Nine other kids headed straight for it.

"The policeman wanted to put him out. But we let him stay. Worse things have happened."

One-eye Connolly, the late, great international gate crasher was what might be called a worst thing. Izzie Silverstein caught him at an Armory wrestling match, "trying to pull the glove trick," a trick, which, to save Izzie trouble, had best go unexplained.

Running a box office is no racket for a man with slow reflexes, weak eyes or peptic ulcers. Izzie Silverstein, free of all these maladies, thinks nothing of dishing out 1,000 ducats in the hour and a half his box office is usually open before a show begins.

That's 10 a minute, and considerably more than 10 in some minutes, and Izzie Silverstein takes it calm and smooth and with a smile. Even with the suspicious people.

"About every other person in the line figures I'm trying to give him a bad seat—you know, saving all the good seats. I don't save out any seats. There's no percentage in that. But try to convince people!"

Every now and then, Izzie Silverstein looks up from selling tickets in the store, and there is Jack Dempsey or Vaughn Moore or some wrestler. The hat show has become, in 26 years, a rendezvous for performers who have a natural interest in how the tickets are going.

Izzie Silverstein is probably the only man in town who sells shirts with a size 20 neck. For wrestlers.

And the tickets, by the way, are usually going fine.

She Uses Newspaper As Pulpit, Pen As Voice In Anti-Hate War

July 12, 1956

S HE BELIEVES THAT LOVE IS STRONGER THAN HATE, that simple Christianity is the strongest force of all, and that we, indeed, are our brothers' keepers.

So every week or so, there is a letter to the editor in *The News'* Public Platform signed "Mrs. Mayme Barger."

She knows perfectly well that many people skip over her letters, and that many people who read them find them silly and naive.

"But they do some good in the world," she says. "I honestly believe my letters help some people along the way.

"Do you remember my piece on Mother's Day? You probably don't, but I worked hard on it. And an old lady from out in the country called me and said her two daughters had been just as mean as they could be to her, but they read my letter and they were being nicer now ...

"I don't know how long I've been writing to the *News.* My husband died 30 years ago; he was a steelworker. I wrote a little news column for the *Monroe Journal* for 12 years ...

"But 23 years ago, I was in an automobile wreck and I haven't been able to work since then. I wrote a religious piece and sent it to *The News* years ago, and I've been doing it ever since.

"Some of the things I write aren't good enough, and I save them and work on them. I know the ones I send help some, because I'm always getting letters and calls from people ... "

Mrs. Mayme Barger is no Plato or Augustine or Schweitzer. She is just Mrs. Mayme Barger, and you can call her gentle letters naive and silly if you want to, stuck there as they are amid the harsh noises and irritations of the rest of the editorial page, just sitting there week after week, repeating things like "Don't be bad to one another," and "Parents, help your children to grow up right."

You can think what you want to, that's your business.

As for Mrs. Mayme Barger, she just thinks maybe we have forgotten those things, and that we ought not to, and that we ought to start remembering them again.

The Stranger At The Station Was Searching, But What For?

July 13, 1956

IT WASN'T ONE OF THOSE "PARDON ME, SIR, but could you spare a dime" things at all. It was more of a conversation in the sun beside the Southern Station, more of a monologue, really.

He leaned the stump of his leg that wasn't there against the grip of one of his crutches and pivoted back and forth one time so he could look both ways down the track.

"It's a hot day, mate," he said.

His voice was a stopper, a voice you couldn't just say, "It sure is," and go your way.

"I left the Windy City on July the fifth, and I got here July the seventh," he said, as if it were the next logical thing to say. "I have been looking this whole day for a maiden aunt of mine who loves in this city. I haven't seen her since 1943."

His eyes were bloodstained brown, not red, and his chin

had a tough stubble on it.

"I'm not from around here, mate. I did work here for seven years in a grocery store when I was nothing but a kid, and I have been looking for that grocery store just casually, you know, and I can't even find it.

"No, I was born and brought up in Baltimore, Maryland. I was on the West Coast last month, out there with the Golden Gate, and I am going back there just as soon as I can. You know, people out there know how to live."

He moved over a few feet, under the shade of the long shed beside he tracks. He took off his old felt hat and wiped the sweat off his head.

"Aw, I don't know," he said. "Mate, I just don't know. If I could find my aunt, I might settle down here for a while, but I'm beginning to think I ain't ever going to find her.

"As a matter of fact, I don't know what I'm going to do next. You ever come to situation like that? There are damn few places I haven't been …

"I was in the Ninety-Second Division during the war, and I have a few friends here and there. I ran into one of them out there on the West Coast, and he didn't even give me the time of day.

"And I'll tell you something else, mate. I was going to try to hit you for a sandwich, but I'll tell you what: To hell with it."

He dropped the stump of his leg down and grabbed the grip of his crutch and swung himself away across the parking lot. "Just to hell with it," he said.

He went around the corner toward the Square, as if his maiden aunt might be in that direction, looking for a sandwich or a ticket to the Golden Gate, looking for a grocery store. Looking for something, anyway.

Petunias Find Haven Among Whizzing Cars

July 16, 1956

S.C. ALEXANDER LIVES IN A HOUSE BY THE SIDE OF THE ROAD, and here's the kind of man he is:

He is the kind of man who can sit in a chair under the big oak trees in his yard and feed the squirrels from his hand.

He is the kind of man who is always giving the neighborhood youngsters nickels to take to the store, and helping them fix their bicycles and giving them a drink of water at the back door.

And he is the only man in Mecklenburg County who ever thought of planting petunias in a traffic island.

The state highway people put the island in front of his big, white house at the intersection of Albemarle Rd. and Delta Rd.

It had a "Stop" sign and a "Keep Right" sign and a reflector pole, but it looked a little bare to S.C. Alexander.

So he planted if full of petunias.

Twice a day, he fills two buckets with water and he waters them. Every few days, he pulls out the weeds.

"The new state highway man told me this was the prettiest traffic island in the state," Mr. Alexander said.

"And you would be surprised how many folks stop—perfect strangers you understand—to find out who keeps the flowers up."

S.C. Alexander keeps the flowers up. For no reason, he said, "except that a lot of people pass that spot and many of them never pass it again, and he thought some of those people might be pleased by the idea of petunias in a traffic island."

That's the kind of man he is.

Joe Pepper Is Second-Story Man With Honest Occupation

July 17, 1956

Y OU CAN SEE THE LADY'S POINT.

There she was, etherized, in her room on the second floor of Cabarrus Hospital. She had just been through a pretty serious operation, so naturally, when she came out of the ether she was a little jumpy.

Her bleary gaze roamed over to the window.

And there, outside her room, was a man.

She screamed.

The man disappeared.

Doctors, interns and nurses scrambled for the ground.

Joe Pepper, window cleaner, just rubbed his bruised shoulder and sighed.

"I didn't think there was anybody in the room," he said. "She scared me so bad, I just let go."

If Joe Pepper wasn't a philosophical guy, that experience might have led him to turn in his squeegee and find a job on *terra firma*.

"But it's all in a day's work," he says. "You gotta expect things like that."

Climbing around buildings runs in the family. Joe is

employed by his father, Doc Pepper, who used to hang by a strap from windows of the Empire State Building before he came to Charlotte and set up City Window Cleaning Company.

During the war, when good window men were hard to come by, even Joe's sister got into the act.

The Cabarrus caper would never have happened had there been hooks for safety straps in the building, Joe says. Only a few Charlotte buildings have hooks, and that makes the job tougher.

"And I wouldn't trust half the hooks in town anyway," Joe adds. "We never washed windows over at the old telephone building on Caldwell, but what one came out of the mortar.

"When they put up the new Jefferson Standard Building, I could have hugged 'em. They got good, strong hooks. So? So they decided to wash their own windows."

Once, Joe was walking around on a Wilder Building ledge (without hooks) when he felt the sash cracking. He dived inside the room—and watched the sash, window and all go crashing to the sidewalk.

Joe, philosophical to a fault, says: "That's one we didn't have to wash."

Joe Pepper started work at 15. His first job was on the then brand new Barring Building.

And when will his last job be?

Again, the shrug.

"Leave us not talk about that."

Peter Gamm's Activities Range From Chess To Cello To Coins

July 18, 1956

THE GUY WHOSE 12-YEAR-OLD FASCINA-TIONS never strayed beyond toads, kites, centerfielders and Phil Harris records was heard to sigh briefly upon meeting Peter Gamm.

Peter, 12, the son of Mr. and Mrs. E.H. Gamm, 226 W. 10th St., likes centerfielders all right, though he's a catcher himself. He definitely prefers Mendelssohn to toads, however, and likes Homer's brand of doggerel better than Harris's.

Last week, as the youngest member of the new Myers Park Symphonette, he conscientiously sawed away at Mendelssohn on a cello, which was not quite bigger than he was, but almost.

"I like Dvorak, too," he said, "especially the Third Concerto."

He was going to a music school when he leaves Harding High, then?

"Oh no," he said. "I'm going to Massachusetts Institute of

Technology. I like astronomy and chemistry. I have a chemistry set and I hope to get a telescope this summer. Chemistry is what I'm really interested in."

Was there anything else he was interested in?

"Sure. Dinosaurs. I saw a dinosaur skeleton at the Smithsonian Institution in Washington.

"I like tropical fish. I've got two aquariums, er, aquaria, and I've got guppies and zebra fish and five white clouds. They're named for the White Cloud mountains in China. I collect stamps, too.

"I've got about 360 coins, mostly American, and if I had four more quarters, I'd have a complete set of quarters from 1927 to 1956. I've got about 3,500 stamps, and I like to read science fiction books, too. I've read all the library's. They've got about 15 or 20. My favorite is by Robert Heinlein, 'The Rolling Stones.' I like stories about the sea, too. I'd like to know some foreign language. Last summer, I learned some German. You've got to know some for chemistry, but I've forgotten it all now. I was going to play the cello in 'The Mikado' at Myers Park Presbyterian Church, but I'm going to New York instead. I'm going to the beach up there. I play chess, too. Mr. Goodwin, who is about 60 or 65 or so comes over to my house and we play on the porch, and I try to learn from him. I taught myself from a book. I don't know why in the world you want to know all this stuff. I hope I don't sound like I'm bragging."

Not at all, not at all, said the guy with the misspent youth. May your cello be mellow, your days long and your quarter collection complete. And would you sign your name on this old piece of copy paper please? I'd like to be able to prove I knew you when.

"When what?" Peter Gamm said. "And by the way, that Homer I read was a simplified version, of course."

Yeah, the ex-12-year-old said, of course.

To Some, Walking City Streets Is Tiring; To Bob, It's A Joy

July 19, 1956

I RODE THE TRAIN," Bob Van Witzenburg said, "and I got out in Charlotte and jumped up in the air. I said, 'Bob, you're here.' And I was, boy!"

To those who do not know Bob Van Witzenburg and the epic story of his desire to simply live in Charlotte, N.C., this may sound like a strenuous greeting to the old town.

So pull up a chair:

"I got here in 1949," Bob Van Witzenburg will tell you. "As a student, you understand, from Holland. My student visa had run out and I had to go back.

"So I just got on a boat and went. It's 3,843 miles from New York to Rotterdam, and all the way, I kept saying, 'Bob, you've got to get back to Charlotte' "

As soon as he reached The Hague, he turned in his application to return as an immigrant.

"Fifteen months later, I heard from them. The American authorities said, 'We'll send you in as a refugee.' I said, 'Bob, you've got yourself a good deal.'

"So I got on the boat and I got to New York. I was the first one off the boat. The man took one look at my passport and he said, 'Boy, where in the world do you think you're going?' This passport is for people who were in Holland during the floods of 1953. You were in the United States in 1953.'

"I looked back across the water and I said, 'Bob, you're going back.' "

They gave him a "Notice To Alien Detained For Inquiry."

"I sat down. A policeman sat down beside me. I went to a hotel and went to sleep. The policeman slept in the next bed, I went down to the inquiry and the policeman went with me. I said, 'Bob, it looks bad.' "

At the inquiry, they told him they were sorry, but his residence had to be the Netherlands in 1953.

Bob Van Witzenburg saw a hole in the big wall: " 'My residence WAS the Netherlands,' I said. 'I was just a student here.' They thought about that a while and they said, 'Okay. Approved.' "

Bob Van Witzenburg walked down the streets of Charlotte this week. Old Central High schoolmates stopped him three times in one Tryon St. block.

He's living in the YMCA, looking for a family to move in with, looking also for a job. He's not worried about finding them.

Seven thousand, six hundred and eighty-six miles is too far to go to worry about anything.

"Bob," Bob Van Witzenburg said. "You're a lucky son of a gun."

Cameras Get Logarithmic Chart; Viewers Get Beautiful Barbara

July 20, 1956

T HIS, KIDDIES, IS A RETMA LOGARITHMIC REFRACTION CHART.

There is not much you can do for a Retma Logarithmic Refraction Chart except point a color TV camera at it for testing.

At least that's what all the WBTV engineers thought until Barbara Bender came along.

She sings in color.

Only about 320 people see her sing in color, because that's about how many people can afford color TV sets. For those who can't, she obligingly sings in black and white.

She comes from Rock Hill, and sings fine.

She likes Bach and Bartok, Sinatra and Fitzgerald.

She used to be in summer stock in Vermont and sing with a band in Washington.

She's really for looking at, not for talking about.
You will pardon us, won't you, if we stop talking?

Earhart, Barkley, Willard, Farley: Names Are Memories For Douglas

July 23, 1956

SELWYN HOTEL, Charlotte, N.C., Att: Douglas."

That's the way letters often arrive from old Selwyn customers. When they do, they go to George Walker Douglas, master of the reservation, the banquet table and the suitcase.

He has been a Selwyn porter since 1928, and he has not missed a day of work in that time, and he

has concluded that the world is full of all kinds of people, and that most kinds are good.

All of the North Carolina governors have known George Walker Douglas, and Vice President Alben Barkley and presidential sidekick Jim Farley and Gen. George Marshall have witnessed his way with a tray.

"I was the bellman for Mr. Jess Willard when he was

here," George Walker Douglas says, and his reminiscing eyes stretch back down the years to the time when the Selwyn interior was dark and cool, after the fashion of the 1930's, and Mr. Jess Willard and his two famous sons were guests.

"I waited on Miss Amelia Earhart," he remembers. And he stood in the lobby months later and watched the traveling citizens reading the newspapers with the big, black headlines about Miss Amelia Earhart.

"I recall I waited on John Dillinger's father," he says. "That was after Dillinger was killed and his father was making lectures around the country about how his son wasn't really bad. That was a sad man, John Dillinger's father."

He waited, too, on Elliott Dexter, a swash-buckling hero of the silent films, the husband of Geraldine Farrar, and, on all the old Confederates, who came here the year they built the Armory Auditorium, for the Confederate Reunion.

"But best of all, I like to remember waiting on Edgar Lee Masters," George Walker Douglas says.

"He lived here for about two years, you know, in the 40's, and he wouldn't have anybody else wait on him.

"I used to take a chair over to the First Presbyterian Church yard and set it in a sunny place and he would sit there and watch the people go by and talk to me.

"Or sometimes, he would sit here in the lobby and when he wanted something he would pound his cane on floor and shout, 'Douglas!' and I would come running."

George Walker Douglas has not become rich in 28 years of answering to his last name. But there are compensations for that: Nobody in town knew Edgar Lee Masters as he did, and few knew Mr. Jose Willard or Miss Amelia Earhart as well, and when the letters come marked, "Att: Douglas," there is only one man they mean.

Young Girl Brings Freshness To Charlotte's Saddest Spot

July 24, 1956

M ORE THAN ANY OTHER PLACE IN MIDTOWN, the cemetery behind the First Presbyterian Church belongs more to other centuries than this one and other men than us.

Its time-worn sidewalks circle the shade of old trees. In the few places where the limbs part and allow splotches of sun to break out on the grass, the sun is unwelcome. It is too bright.

The cemetery belongs to "Catherine Peel, Who Departed This Life May Ye 24th, 1778," and to the Hon. William Davidson and Maj. Gen. George Graham and Octavia Elizabeth Jones.

Carol, however, didn't understand this.

Carol did not respect the sad spirit of the place, because being only six, she did not feel it. She came into the cemetery holding the hand of her father. It was a gray day, the sun was behind a cloud, the old men on the bench in the corner of the lot talked quietly and aimlessly, passing the time.

But Carol, being only six, ran down the sidewalks, looked at the curious, ornate tombstones and pierced the musty soul of the place with her laughter.

"Carol," her father said, "try not to be too noisy, now."

She tried, but it was a losing attempt.

She swung around an oak tree ("Planted In Honor Of The Visit Of Gen. George Washington To Charlotte, N.C., May, 1791") and stood upon a bench to get a better view and scared a stuffy pigeon when she jumped down.

"This is a funny place, Daddy," Carol said. "I like it."

The old men feeding the squirrels in a corner of the cemetery looked up and smiled at her. The sun, by coincidence or design, came out from behind its cloud.

"Daddy," Carol said, "what does it say on this one?"

What it said was, "Mary Long Davidson, Who Departed This Life June 27, 1802, In The Sixth Year Of Her Age."

Her father read it and smiled at her. He took her by the hand and they walked through the gate on to 5th St.

The old men went back to talking. The benches, the graves, the old sidewalks were just as they were before she came.

Nothing was different.

For five minutes, the little girl breathed freshness and youth into the cemetery's air, a task unequal to any but a six-year-old.

"You don't ever see many kids in here," one of the old men said.

Carol disappeared down the street, and the cemetery behind First Presbyterian Church went back to being the oldest, saddest place in town.

An Assault At Latta Arcade:
Sunshine Brings Shenanigans

July 25, 1956

IT WAS A NICE, bright day with the sun beating down on Latta Arcade, warming the plate glass windows of the brokers ánd lawyers and real estate men and peeking in on a conspiracy brewing on the bench near Church St.

The oldest conspirator was maybe 12.

"Wait'll somebody comes by, see," he said.

"Okay," the middle one said.

"Then," the oldest one said, "you grab me around the neck and pull me down and I'll hit you a couple of times."

The middle one laughed.

"It'll work great," he said.

The littlest one butted in: "What am I going to do?"

"You act like you're trying to get us apart," the middle one said.

"Or just sit there and look worried," the oldest one said.

"Act like you're crying," the middle one suggested.

"How do you do that?"

"Just look worried," the oldest one said.

They sat on the bench and looked both ways down the arcade, and in a few minutes a little gray-haired lady with a big pocketbook came walking along.

"Okay," the oldest one whispered. "Let's go."

The middle one hollered, "Okay, boy, you asked for it!" and pulled the oldest one off the bench.

The oldest one hit him in the belly. They both groaned. They rolled over and over on the sidewalk, and the little old lady stopped.

"Goodness gracious," she said.

The littlest one forgot to look worried and just grinned at the lady behind her back. She didn't see him. She started to walk past, but she couldn't. Her mother's heart wouldn't let her.

"You boys!" she said. "Stop that!"

The littlest one giggled.

The little old lady walked right up to the two boys struggling against the wall and hollered, "You boys should find some other ways to settle your differences."

The oldest one groaned again and sank back against the wall.

The middle one, who didn't know what was coming, recovered in time to stand up, dust himself off and say, "That ought to hold him."

The littlest one giggled again and the middle one smirked. The oldest boy bounced up and started laughing.

The old lady tightened her lips and walked off down the arcade.

The three boys just sat on the bench and laughed.

It was a nice, bright, sunshiny day, and they were more than a match for any old lady who happened along, and if their luck held up there would be another one along any minute.

Bill Condos Left Tito, Ike, Caviar For Tryon St. And Cheeseburgers

July 26, 1956

IN THREE FAST MONTHS, Bill Condos has forsaken champagne for coffee, caviar for cheeseburgers and kings, generals and dictators for office girls and plain S. Tryon St. Joes.

This sounds like a crazy transaction, but there is an explanation for it:

Bill Condos had gone just about as far as he could in his line of work without crossing an ocean.

So, in May, he turned in his white tie to the manager of the King George Hotel (Greece's largest) and caught the next boat for the USA. Next thing he knew, he was serving up black coffee and cherry pie to the citizens on the Pink House stools.

His friend and employer, Nick Hondros, also acts as interpreter when the English gets too thick for comfort.

Leaving out the interpretation, the conversation goes like this:

"When did you get here?"

"Tenth of May."

"Ever meet any interesting people?"

"Sure, Eisenhower."

(He whips out a picture of Condos, wearing a tuxedo, and Ike, wearing five stars, both smiling.)

"Anybody else?"

"Sure, Tito, Adenauer, Montgomery, Marilyn Maxwell, Haile Selassie."

"Don't you miss rubbing shoulders with famous people?"

(Condos and Hondros go into complicated Greek conversation. Nick comes out of it with an answer.)

"He says he's working his way up. He figures he'll see 'em all again in New York someday."

"Did you know anybody else?

"Sure, Onassis."

"Onassis? The Greek ship owner? The fabulous yachtsman? The world's richest man?"

"Sure."

"What's he like?"

(Another lengthy conversation. Nick comes up with the word again.)

"He says, 'Kovardas.' "

(Ah, insight into the anatomy of wealth.)

"What's that mean?"

"Good tipper," Nick said.

It's Time For The Roundup: Shelton Still Collects, And So Does John

July 27, 1956

Remember George Anton, who left his 4th St. grill for greener pastures, only to yield to popular demand and come back?

They painted a sign on his window: "George Is Back!"

There's another sign there now. It says "(Try To) Eat Breakfast With Greasy George. Contains Lanolin."

They love him on 4th St.

In the mail, a postcard from Shelton Hutchison, the amazing preacher who collects. Anything. He has music boxes, coats of arms, buttons, stamps, coins, rocks, accordions (and 20 other musical instruments), yardsticks, fossils and books of Hebrew and Greek.

The postcard came from Switzerland. And what did it say?

"Have found two trunks of interesting things."

The "Governor," Tryon Street's loudest and proudest news vendor, whose real name is Eugene Broughton, wants it known that he is, too, related to the late Gov. J. Melville.

"Not much kin there, but a little bit," the Governor said, in his temperate tone, the one that can be heard only from

Thacker's to the middle of the next block.

And PEOPLE helped line the pocket of John Clifford. He's the 17-year-old Houdini whose specialty is escaping from a straitjacket while hanging from a fire ladder.

The day after the story about John appeared, he pulled his escape act on the Oasis floor show. Two muscular citizens from the audience roped him in, and two minutes later he was free.

Whereupon, the two abashed gents offered him $25 if he could do it again outside.

But this time, they strapped him into the jacket in unorthodox fashion. They tied the ropes around his shoulder. They put his arms in backwards. They pulled it tight.

It was impossible to escape.

They thought.

Houdini Clifford collected his 25 bucks in 2 minutes, 20 seconds.

Three Years Of Hard Work Will Disappear In Sky (He Hopes)

July 30, 1956

THERE IS DRAMA IN THE STORY OF JIMMY BLACKSTONE and his six-foot rocket. There is high adventure. There is the lure of the skies.

"There is," Jimmy adds, "a pretty good chance that the thing will just blow up."

If it does, it won't be because of any lack of figuring, measuring, joining, shaping, hammering and welding on Jimmy's part.

For three years, off and on, he has worked on the rocket. He has brought all his 17-year-old ingenuity to its construction. He has read everything he could get his hands on, he has had the professional advice and assistance of Dr. Herbert Hechenbleikner, director of science teaching in city schools, and of the Aluminum Company of America. He has tolled and sweated over drawing boards and construction charts.

In a couple of weeks, he's going to lug his rocket out into the country, fill it with pressurized gasoline and liquid oxygen, and press the button.

"I don't know what will happen then," he says. "If you figure it out mathematically, it'll go maybe a mile high."

Just in case mathematics fails him, he's going to launch the monster from a deep hole and from as great a distance as possible.

It isn't that Jimmy (the son of Mr. and Mrs. Burt Blackmon, 1815 Club Rd.) isn't confident. He's just scientifically judicious.

He can talk about his slender brainchild all day, in terms like these:

"The nose is a $5 lampshade. Each of the tanks has its own valves and gauges, of course. The combustion chamber is six inches long and two inches in diameter. Temperature inside it will reach about 3,000 degrees centigrade, so I had to install a dry ice cooling system to keep the aluminum from melting. The launching platform will have two guide rails pitched at a slight angle ... "

When the juice hits the chemicals, the fledgling V-12's career will be over, no matter whether it reaches Arcturos or merely covers an acre of Mecklenburg with little pieces of aluminum.

Jimmy Blackmon's three-year hopes will be riding on his lampshade nose.

And *The Charlotte News* will be there for the big whoom. Jimmy has agreed to that.

"Just bring your own brick wall," he said, "to get behind."

Friends Quit (What Ain't Dead), But Farmer Tarleton Holds Fast

July 31, 1956

I GOT SQUASH AND OKRA AND GOOD FRESH CORN," W.D. Tarleton said.

That's the story of his life.

"It's all home growed," he said. "I don't buy a thing."

It's all home growed on the farm not far from Matthews, just as it has been for 35 years. Tuesdays and Fridays, he sells it on Thomas Ave. in Midwood. The rest of the time, he worries with it, watches the sky, pulls the weeds.

"I'm the last one around here selling vegetables from a truck," W.D. Tarleton will tell you. "There's plenty of them go down to Columbia and buy it, and there used to be a good many growed their own. But I'm the last.

"What ain't dead done quit."

W.D. Tarleton used to have some help.

"I still have an old colored man who's too old to do anything," he says. "But my son left me and joined the Army. Decided he'd rather fight than farm, and I can't blame him.

"I might quit myself if I had the choice, but I don't.

"I got bell pepper, hot pepper, tomatoes, cucumber, peas and good green beans," he says. "Picked yesterday, and two pounds of these peas will shell out to one pound easy."

The economics, the supermarkets and the weather are all against W.D. Tarleton, and his friends in the business (what ain't dead) have quit, and his son has joined the Army.

But the vegetables are fresh and firm, the Thomas Ave. shade is cool.

There are worse ways to make a living, and hundreds of less honorable ways than to sell two days a week two pounds of peas which you know very well will shell out to one pound, at least.

August 1956

He was a fun guy to be with, had a great sense of humor. He liked to have a good time, but his idea of a good time was talking about newspapers and journalism more than anything else. You always knew that Charlie's main focus was on his career and newspapering.

—Erwin Potts,
reporter, *Charlotte News*

Lass Learns Harsh Fact Of Life: Most Wishes Have Price Tags

August 1, 1956

SHE WALKED SLOWLY ALONG THE DIME STORE COUNTER, stopping at almost every step to pick up a toy, to fly an airplane in her hand, to turn the pulp pages of a coloring book.

The salesgirl leaned against the counter at one end, idly watching her.

She bumped against a boy on her way down the counter, looked up in surprise, passed him and went on, examining every toy in the display.

She passed by the water pistols, picked up a card of jacks as if she had never seen jacks before, looked at them silently for a while, passed on to the rubber balls, the bows and arrows and the metal autos.

At the very end of the counter were the dolls. When she

reached them, she stopped.

She stood with her hands at her sides and just looked at the dolls.

One of them was a blonde with a frilly pink dress and red cheeks and blue eyes and eyelids that closed. She had a blue bow in her hair and blue laces on her shoes.

The little girl finally reached up and touched the patent leather shoes, and touched the pink dress. She did not pick up the doll, she just looked at it.

The salesgirl moved her way with a bored look on her face. The little girl walked over to her and said, "How much is she?"

She did not say "it," she said "she."

The salesgirl flipped over the price tag.

"Seven ninety-five," she said.

The little girl held her hand up towards the salesgirl. It held a dime, a nickel and three pennies.

The salesgirl laughed. "No, that ain't seven ninety-five," she said.

The little girl looked at her.

"That ain't enough," the salesgirl said.

The little girl touched the doll's shoes again and looked into the staring eyes that were too blue to be true.

"Now, you go home and get your seven dollars and 77 cents. Or," the salesgirl said, "you can buy some paper dolls ... "

The little girl didn't hear her. She started around the counter, stopped, and walked toward the door of the store, with her coins in her hand and with tears in her eyes for the blonde and blue-eyed piece of beauty that 18 cents couldn't buy.

Whistler Added A New Dimension To The Gray Trade St. Morning

August 2, 1956

It WAS A GRAY MORNING YESTER-DAY, a depressing, overcast one, and the mist settled down on the city, swirled in the dingy Trade St. doorways, and the sadness of it all touched the newspaper vendors and the yawning waitresses and got in your breakfast coffee.

At 7 a.m., it was a day without any promise on Trade St. A shabby woman shifted from one foot to another in front of the bus station, walked inside to look at the clock, as if the time made a great deal of difference to her particular plans for the day.

Across the street, two red-faced citizens sat on the low Post Office wall, one drunker than the other. At 7:30 or 8 or 8:30, if they stayed there, they would be collared by a day-shift officer, his first arrest of the long day, and the time made no difference at all to them.

Even the cars, moving along Trade St. sang a sad song,

their tires drying out the damp pavement. The traffic lights stopped blinking yellow and started their 18-hour automatic clicking to red and green, as well.

There wasn't any hope for the day at all, at 7 a.m.

So why was he whistling?

Why was he, a gray-haired, tieless man with a lunch bag, who looked as if he had as many troubles as the next guy, walking along in front of the First Presbyterian Church whistling, of all things, "It's A Big, Wide, Wonderful World"?

The words of that song go, in part:

"Life is a mystic, a midsummer's night, you live in a Turkish delight, you're in heaven ... "

Those were inappropriate sentiments, to say the least, at 7 o'clock yesterday morning, so why did the sadness that touched everything else on Trade St. skip over him?

Why did he stop, reach into his paper sack and come out with a bag of peanuts, and toss them through the iron railings of the fence to the squirrels and pigeons?

Answer this: What was so mystic about life that led him to whistle on a day like that?

What was Turkish, or delightful, about walking on a dirty sidewalk in front of the Presbyterian church?

And why, when he and his whistling ("You're the master of all you survey, you're a gay Santa Claus") had faded around the Church St. corner, why did his echo hang in the air, why were the corny lyrics almost believable, why did it look as though there might be something to the day after all?

Answer that.

John Kelly Wall's Okay, But He Can't Cut Flips Like Blackjack

August 3, 1956

T HIS STARTED OUT TO BE ABOUT JOHN KELLY WALL, a friendly and accomplished officer of the law, who has many interesting experiences under his Sam Browne belt and much to recommend him to the reading public.

That was before he started talking about his cat.

True Police Adventures are as nothing beside John Kelly Wall's cat, Blackjack.

Blackjack is (1) one of Mecklenburg's biggest, 18 pounds when stark naked, which he always is, (2) one of Mecklenburg's blackest, the color of a coal mine at three o'clock in the morning, and (3) the only cat in Mecklenburg County that is listed for taxes.

"He's pure alley bred," John Kelly Wall says. "Well, not

exactly. He was bred in a cornfield down below the house. His parents were full blooded. He was a throwback somewhere along the line."

Right away, Blackjack proved himself no ordinary cat. While most kittens get a little snarlish after so many hours of maltreatment from children, Blackjack submitted to every torture in the book from the start. For eight years, the Wall back yard has been a sort of neighborhood nursery, play-ground and ball field, and Blackjack has been nurse, keeper and left fielder.

"His favorite trick is jumping to your shoulder and cutting a flip backwards out of your hand," John Kelly Wall says.

Blackjack does it all day. Friends walk into the yard, strangers, brush salesmen—Blackjack jumps to their shoul-ders, cuts a flip backwards.

"I took Hinson (Patrolman R.G.) home with me one day," John Kelly Wall remembers. "Liked to scared him to death."

Patrolman Wall started thinking about this one time and decided that Blackjack was such a commodity as should be on the tax books.

"If he got run over or something and I tried to prove I owned him and there was no tax record, according to the law there'd be no cat," he says. And there WAS a cat. Was there ever a cat!

So John Kelly Wall went down and listed Blackjack for $25 on the county tax books, the first county cat ever given such a distinction, as far as anybody knows.

John Kelly Wall is a nice enough guy, but he never cut a flip from a brush salesman's shoulder in his life.

Here's his picture. We'll tell you about him some day.

Will Power Helped, And The Cap Stayed On His Trans-Atlantic Coke

August 6, 1956

W HEN ARNOLD L. HILL ENLISTED in the Air Corps in October, 1942, his mama bought a couple of Cokes at the A&P and put them in his suitcase.

"You'll probably want one on your way to Richmond," she said.

He did. But he figured there might come a time when he'd want one more. He left the two bottles in his barracks during basic training.

He took them to Camp Kilmer, N.J., transferred them to a duffle bag, and rode on the boat to England with them.

Over there, a buddy got sick, offered him a dollar for one of them, and Arnold L. Hill gave it to him

"When the guys found out I had another Coke, they started bidding for it," he says. "They offered me a lot of money, but I fought 'em off. I told them I might crack it open when the war was over."

That Coca-Cola, with "Charlotte, N.C.," embossed on the bottom, went across the English Channel into France in 1944. When Arnold L. Hill's fighter-bomber group went into Germany in 1945, the Coke went, too.

"When the war ended, I just figured since I'd kept it that long, I'd hang on to it a little while longer," its owner says. It went into a duffle bag and came back to Charlotte.

Arnold L. Hill got married, found himself a house on Hilltop Circle near Derita, and settled down to being a postman. The Coke went on the shelf.

Weaker men would have reached for the bottle opener years ago, and Arnold L. Hill, who has been thirsty a few times since 1942, has thought about it. He has looked at it, touched it, and thought about it.

But he's got will power running out of his ears. And a 14-year-old Coca-Cola with a rusty bottle cap to prove it.

From Ships To Seeds Is No Easy Transition For H.W. Ashcraft

August 7, 1956

S ELLING GRASS SEED AND TEN-PENNY NAILS IS NOT EASY for H.W. Ashcraft.

How could it be, for a lean, suntanned, tattooed man who has trod the planks of a hundred ships from Malay to Key West?

For more than 20 years, he was Chief Bos'na Mate Ashcraft, and he sailed all the seven seas, and he put into more ports than he can remember now, behind the counter at Derita Hardware Store.

It's not an unpleasant job. The youngsters in the neighborhood call him "Sinbad the Sailor." He likes the people and the people like him.

But the nearest body of water is Sayer's Lake, and that's what's hard to take.

H.W. Ashcraft never hears from the friends he shipped with as late as two years ago.

"That's a funny thing about sailors," he'll tell you. "They never write. You can be the closest of friends with a man in the Navy, and when you say goodbye to him he'll never write because he figures he'll run into you again sometime."

They won't run into H.W. Ashcraft. He's married and settled down and working in a hardware store.

But in a corner of his house at 1922 Academy St., he has a collection of sailing ships he built himself, carved out of stovewood and fitted, accurately and carefully, with masts and riggings.

"I even put furniture in them," he says. "You can't see it—but I know it's there."

And you know what?

H.W. Ashcraft can't even find anybody in the whole town of Charlotte, N.C., who knows enough about model ships to talk about them.

It's a landlubber's town. You can throw a rock across Sayer's Lake.

Carolyn Had to Get Rid Of Pups But Sidewalk Sales Were Slow

August 8, 1956

N. Tryon Street's shop-
pers jostled the little girl
up against the plate glass
window of McLellan's.
There she stood beside the
penny scales with a puppy
in her hand and two more
puppies in the basket at
her feet.

"Puppy?" she asked.
There were no buyers.

Carolyn Presgrove, 10,
was taking the direct way
of tackling a tough job.

Occasionally, someone
stopped and peered into the basket, where the puppies were
huddled in a heap with their eyes closed.

"What kind are they?" a boy asked.

"Toy terrier, rat terrier and Boston bull," Carolyn
answered.

Each of the puppies, she meant, was all three.

The boy said, "They sure are pretty." He looked decidedly sympathetic.

"How much are they?" he asked.

"Five dollars for a female and seven dollars for a male," Carolyn said.

"That's a lot of money," he said.

"They're worth it, though," Carolyn said.

Why was she holding a sidewalk puppy sale? Carolyn explained it, looking a little sad:

"Daddy said I had to get rid of them. I didn't exactly want to, but we still have Jip—that's their mother—and one dog is enough, Daddy says. Their names are Whitey and St. Bernard and Playful Girl. They're all silly names, I guess, but that's just what I call them. My brother told me how much to charge and where to stand. He said charge ten dollars for males but I came down because nobody was buying males. I've sold two females. My brother is going to buy a rifle with the money, I think."

Carolyn poured a little milk from a half-pint carton into a bowl and offered it to the puppies. One of them stepped into it.

"I think they're scared by the noise around here," Carolyn said.

She picked up Whitey and stroked his neck. Whitey blinked at the passersby, and they stared back curiously.

"Puppy?" Carolyn asked.

Pauper Poet Seeks Reason For Being In Works Of Bobby Burns

August 9, 1956

AT NIGHT, you can find Malcolm Whitt at the Charlotte Rescue Mission, where he lives. In the daytime, you may find him wherever there is a bench he can lean his crutches against and sit down on and summon an audience.

Malcolm Whitt always has an audience. For he is a poet as well as a pauper.

"Good morning, my friend," he will say. "Rest yourself a moment," and he smiles from under his nicotine-stained mustache.

"I have a poem for you," he will say, and launch into one of his favorites, like:

"Falling away
"Like the leaves of a tree
"On an autumn day ... "

"Do you comprehend the deep meaning of that poem, my friend?" he will ask, and if you say no, he will simply say the poem over for you.

Malcolm Whitt says he is a college man ("UNC, 1921")

and troubled by the dark state of the world and by his own inability to exist in it elsewhere than the Charlotte Rescue Mission. ("I was in the County Home for a while, but I found it a crude and disagreeable place," he says, "and so I left.")

Before he lost his leg in an automobile accident, he was a machinist. Now, he passes the days in places like the bench in front of Sears, quoting diverse poets to whoever has a minute listen.

"Time was when the little toy dog was new
"And the soldier was passing fair;
"And that was the time when our little Boy Blue
"Kissed them and put them there."

"Eugene Field," he says. "Wonderful poet. I like David, the Psalmist, a great writer."

"Weeping may endure for a night
"But joy cometh in the morning."

"And Bobby Burns. Oh yes, he was magnificent. Nobody could write like that."

"Man's inhumanity to man
"Makes countless thousands mourn."

"What a powerful thought! Do you understand the powerful thought in that simple line, my friend? In a time when a true Christian is rejected by men, the world would benefit by a full comprehension of that thought, I assure you."

He shifts his big frame on the bench and looks at the sidewalk for a moment.

"Well," he says. "I write verses myself. Here, I have a poem for you ... "

New Arrival From Raleigh Seeks, Solace From Policeman On Corner

August 10, 1956

THE CURIOUS FACT IS that people always in trouble with the law often really like policemen and find a certain amount of pride in knowing one well enough to call him by his first name.

Sometimes, the cop that runs a man in is his only friend in the world.

That may explain why the old lady, five days out of Woman's Prison, was standing on the square telling the policeman her troubles.

"I don't know how many times I've been in jail," she said. "I've just lost count.

"But now that I'm out, I want two things: I want a job and I want my husband's body moved. If they don't move my husband's body from that field over there in Concord to this nice plot I've got in Oaklawn Cemetery, I'm going to move him myself."

The policeman turned from watching the cars go by. "You can't do that, now," he said.

"Well, somebody's got to move him," she said. "It's a disgrace, him lying out in that field. They didn't even give him a half-way decent box."

She had to look up to him in the face, and she waved her hands as she talked.

"I'd have seen to it myself long ago," she said, "but I was in Raleigh. That judge, he thought he was a smart man, and he give me 12 months.

"I figure if you're going to be a prisoner, though, be a prisoner. I got honor grade, badges and everything, and a clean dress every day. And I wrote to the parole board and I told 'em I'd never get drunk again. I wasn't drunk at the time, but that judge didn't want to listen. The police came into the cafe and said I was drunk after ONE BEER, and he give me 12 months."

The policeman nodded and looked away.

"I've worked all around here, at the dairy and the bakery when it was down here on Thrift Rd., and I reckon I've made a thousand sheets for that jail, and I've worked at the mill, and listen:

"Since I got back, I ain't found a single person I know. I've got to get a job. I'm a working woman."

She stopped talking for a minute and just looked at him.

"You reckon I could get my husband moved," she asked.

"Look," he said, "just go down to the station—" He pointed down E. Trade St.

"I know where it is," she said. "It's no use."

"—And tell it to the desk sergeant," he said.

"I don't want to talk to no sergeant," she said. "I want my husband moved. He did get me arrested a couple of times, but ... "

The policeman walked into the center of Tryon St. to move the cars along a little faster, and the old lady stood and watched him for a minute before she shuffled off down N. Tryon, not E. Trade.

September 1956

He had the ability to write about small things and make them big.

—Emery Wister,
entertainment reporter, *Charlotte News.*

He Lost His Castle to The Sea, But Gained A Valuable Lesson

September 3, 1956

W RIGHTSVILLE BEACH—The sun and the tide came up together. The sun burst from behind a bank of low clouds in a sudden, dramatic dawn and the tide, splashing the farthest pilings of the Wrightsville jetties, reversed itself silently and indiscernibly.

Three people watched the sun come up: two fishermen in a boat just beyond the breakers and a boy, an eleven-year-old vacationer, who had just left his parents' cottage to go down and build a castle in the sand.

The red ball of sun attracted the castle-builder's eye for an instant. The turning of the tide passed his notice.

As the sun rose and grew warm, the fishermen took off their shirts. The boy worked on. With a small shovel, he dug a moat in the soft sand. He built a fortified approach and scooped a tunnel entrance through the outer wall. He studded the wall with sea shells for windows.

Then the boy started to work on his tower. He built it nearly three feet tall, broad at the base and pointed at the top. He built it slowly and carefully, for more than an hour, smoothing every inch with his hands.

The fishermen, their net full, beached their boat near the boy's castle. As they dragged the boat up the beach, one of them said, "That's a real nice castle," and the boy smiled at him.

It was a magnificent castle. It was not like a child's work. It was very nearly flawless.

Soon after the fishermen left, the boy finished. He topped the tower's spire with a bright shell and smoothed out the approaching paths. Then he ran to the cottage, brought his mother, father, sister and grandmother out to see what he had done. As they stood and admired it a dying wave fanned within inches of the outer wall.

"The water's not going to get it, is it?" the boy asked.

"Maybe not," his father said.

While his family wandered down the beach, the boy went to work on a tall wall of sand toward the ocean. Suddenly, unexpectedly, a wave broke 20 feet from the wall, foamed over it, broke down the inner wall of the boy's castle and filled the moat.

He rushed to repair the damage. Before he could, the moat filled again. A third wave rushed in and eroded the base of the tower. Half of it sank into mud.

The boy stopped working and stood beside the fishermen's boat watching the destruction. In another ten minutes, he couldn't tell exactly where his castle had been.

"You should have built that one where the tide wouldn't get it." One of the fishermen had come back to hang his net.

The boy nodded. He had learned something about the ocean, something that the fishermen knew all along. He looked down at the broad, smooth beach and at the water of the rising tide surging in brown pools around his bare feet.

For Two Jumpers, Charlotte
Proved A Rugged 'Drop Zone'

September 4, 1956

THEY WERE STANDING ON THE CORNER in the words of the song, watching all the girls go by.

Trouble was, all the girls WERE going by. For the two paratroopers on the Square, it was a real tough Sunday afternoon. There was nobody else to talk to, so they talked to the cop.

"You know any girls who might like a date?" one of them asked.

"Not a chance, soldier," said the policeman.

So they wandered down S. Tryon and back up again, past the sexy marquee of Tryon Theater. They sort of smiled at the girl in the booth. She didn't even change her expression.

They walked up to the Liggett's corner. There were other paratroopers there, and girls. With husbands holding one hand, youngsters holding the other.

"Maybe we ought to go on back," one of them suggested after a while.

"Not," the other one said, "that."

They strolled down the quiet street to Effird's. Lots of pretty girls. In the windows.

In front of the Carolina Theater, they looked at all the pictures of Marilyn Monroe. The movie ended while they were standing there and people started coming out. Including girls.

So the paratroopers, bravely, walked up to the prettiest one, who looked a little like Marilyn herself, a blonde, and one of them said to her bravely, "Hello."

She nodded.

"Would you and maybe a friend like to go out with us?" the paratrooper asked.

"Nope," she said.

"Please ... " the paratrooper started.

"Look," the girl said, "you went to jump school, right?"

"Sure," the paratrooper said, and his buddy, who also went to jump school, came up to join in telling war stories—or something.

"Then go jump in a lake," the girl said.

It was a tough afternoon. That's all you can say for it.

Harry Villeponteaux Was Happy Man Until He Ran Into Sept. 5

September 5, 1956

TAKE IT FROM HARRY VILLEPONTEAUX and stay indoors today. Sept. 5 is for rabbits.

Back in 1930, Harry Villeponteaux was a happy man. He was juggling clubs and hats and clowning for the John Robinson Circus, traveling through the South and Midwest, hitting the harvest territory. One of his best friends on the show was Emmett Kelly, who had a trapeze act. Everything was fine. But the bubble exploded, the crowds stopped coming and the show folded 26 years ago today.

All right. Harry Villeponteaux had had his troubles before, like when in 1924 five elephants jumped out of the stage door of the Wallace Theater in Peru, Ind., and ran right through the middle of town and two of them fell in the Mississinewah River. He shrugged his shoulders and went to work doing balloon ascensions and parachute jumps.

In that line of work Harry Villeponteaux managed to land in the trees, lakes and stockyards and scrape the side of a library.

He was never really in danger, though, until Sept. 5, 1933, when he came down atop 33,000 volts worth of high power lines in Greenfield, Mo. He landed on the middle wire, the only safe one, and bounced over. But he got to wondering about Sept. 5.

By 1952, of course, a lot of Sept. 5's were under the bridge and Harry Villeponteaux was relaxing again. So, in Blakesburg, Iowa, on Sept. 5, an ankle rope broke during a trapeze act. He went to the hospital for 12 weeks, and his career in show business was over.

Now, Harry Villeponteaux works at the Spur Station on Independence Blvd., plays a white-face clown Sundays at Airport Park, drives a Ford with a clown suit, a cotton candy machine and a dozen old *Billboard* magazines in the back seat.

He's got a house in the country. He's keeping in touch with show business. He's hoping someday to open a school for acrobats.

That's someday. Today is Sept. 5, and today, Harry Villeponteaux is keeping both feet on the ground; turning his back on no suspicious characters, driving slowly, and watching the clock.

At midnight, he'll feel better.

No Office, No Stock, No Dividends, But The Partnership Is Unbeatable

September 6, 1956

Today, we would bend your ear with the happy success story of an American capitalistic enterprise: John Williams Cut Flowers.

There are no stockholders in this company because there is no stock. There is no office and no office equipment, not even so much as a typewriter or telephone.

Total assets remain exactly what they were when John Williams Cut Flowers opened for business 18 years ago—two acres of flowers in Paw Creek, a stand to sell them from in Myers Park and a few tin cans.

This is a chaste, simple business that is in no danger of declaring dividends or winning a government contract. There are two officers, just as there have been from the start. They are John Williams, president, and Herbert McDonald, general manager, and they have no bosses and nobody to boss.

The inventory, also, has remained the same for 18 years: sweetpeas and buttercups in the spring, then gladiolas, chrysanthemums, dahlias, bachelor's-buttons, "rooster comb."

The only thing that has changed is the location and that changed this week. John Williams and Herbert McDonald moved their flower stand from the intersection of Providence Road and Queens Road down Queens to Morehead Street, a distance of about three blocks.

John Williams, painting the neat, new stand this week, explained it: "It was the parking situation and the library. People couldn't stop. They'd slow down and see the flowers and the No Parking sign about the same time. I hated to move after 18 years, but people are finding out where we are now."

"I'm glad to be moved," General Manager McDonald said. "I work every day except Sunday and Monday from about 7 in the morning to 6:30 or 7 at night, and most of it lately has been just waiting for somebody to come by. Now, that's work, don't let nobody tell you otherwise. That waiting is worrisome."

John Williams and his general manger are looking forward to a busy autumn. There will be fall flowers to sell and bulbs to put in the two Paw Creek acres, and when spring comes again the business will be 19 years old and not a cent richer.

But when spring comes, you see, the buttercups will bloom. It's an understanding the firm of John Williams Cut Flowers has with nature. It's a little outfit, but you can't beat the partnership.

King W.S. Strong Knows How To Make Diapers Tops For Bottoms

September 7, 1956

Flying high on the flagpole of progress, fluttering coura-geously in the gentle breezes of the Atomic Age, is the diaper. The diaper has come a long way.

The big, square, white cotton diaper flourishes today only among the most rock-ribbed, conservative infants. The "advanced" gauze-type diaper measuring 20 inches by 40 inches from stem to, so to speak, stern, is as obsolete as the abacus.

Diapers are on the march, and the local diaper king is W.S. Strong, owner of Storkline Dy-Dee Wash and national president of the avant garde National Institute of Diaper Services.

"Ninety percent of our customers," Mr. Strong says, "pre-fer the no-fold contour sheet, a good-looking, form-fitting diaper."

Back in the pre-no-fold contour sheet days, grandma, even if she had had one, would probably have just put it on the baby. That's not the way it's done.

After washing the diaper, Mr. Strong's company treats it with an antiseptic solution. "This renders it absolutely clean," he says. And not just for the present, either. The diaper goes out ready to kill any germs which happen on it before it gets where it's going.

Then, the diaper gets a dose of textile softener, whatever that is, and a shot of deodorant. Every week or so, a sample diaper goes off to a U.S. Testing Service laboratory, just to make sure everything is working right.

Then, the diaper goes on the baby, secured by two super-safe, stainless steel safety pins. Right away, of course, it comes off again and goes through the whole withering process once more.

"Our big enemy," Mr. Strong says, "is the washing machine. People think they can get diapers clean in a washing machine."

The tone of his voice implied what he thought of that notion. "They just can't," he said.

Mr. Strong's company washes a staggering number of diapers, five million a year. His trucks deliver them and pick them up.

"All the customer needs," he says, "is the baby."

How's THAT for an Atomic Age motto?

That Drummer Had The Beat Even If The Roof Caved In

September 10, 1956

IN THE MIDDLE OF PANDEMONIUM, he never changed expression.

It was convocation time at the House of Prayer, Daddy Grace was in town, the preachers were preaching, the singers were singing, everybody was dancing.

He was in the corner, 10 years old at the outside, beating out a steady, driving, practiced rhythm on a snare drum.

Four trombone players were aiming their horns at his ear and blaring out for all they were worth. Two English horn players were sweating hard. The deafening sound ricocheted around the room.

The drummer tapped his foot, ever so slightly, tried a couple of rim shots and looked around serenely, as if he were playing a practice pad on a South Sea island instead of laying down a blazing beat for the biggest event of the year on S. McDowell St.

You looked at him, and you couldn't believe it. From his wrists up, nothing moved. You couldn't even see his drumsticks, they were flashing so fast.

He was terrific. He was calm and relaxed and professional

and nonchalant and terrific, and he never missed a beat. He never changed expression.

Shades, you thought, of Pan and Toscanini and Zutty Shingleton and everything that has ever been worth listening to in this world.

From the sound of things, the roof was coming in. If it had, he'd have been there in the rubble, playing riffs.

You never found out his name. And you never forgot the beat.

Lon Smith Made Up For Lost Time With Sunday School Class

September 11, 1956

LON SMITH GOT STARTED Sunday School teaching a little late. He was 31 years old when he first took the International Sunday School lesson in his hands and taught it to a class at a mission of the Tryon St. Methodist Church.

That was in 1907, and Lon Smith has made up for lost time. The little mission has expanded into the large Belmont Park Methodist Church, the Sunday School has expanded to 1,000 members. Mr. Smith, who was 80 years old last week, is still at it.

They had a "Lon Smith Day" at the church last month, the sort of thing that is usually reserved for ball players and politicians or others in the public eye. Sunday School teachers generally don't qualify. But Lon Smith is no ordinary Sunday School teacher.

Emmett Jerome, once a member of Mr. Smith's class and now mayor of Rock Hill, S.C., came back to make a speech.

And H.H. Hall, the president of the Sunday School, remarked: "There's nobody like Mr. Smith, not in our church. I don't know what we'd do without him."

"Mr. Smith is just the best teacher I've ever run across," a member of the Men's Bible Class said. "To tell you the truth, he's better than most preachers."

Lon Smith, starting his 50th year as a Sunday School teacher after that slow start in 1907, has a few observations about the job. You can put them down as the words of a man who ought to know what he's talking about.

"The four gospels go over better with people than other parts of the Bible. I enjoy the old books for their history, but people perk up to Matthew, Mark, Luke and John, because they're familiar with the subject.

"Despite the evidence of people ignoring the Bible nowadays, I think as a great a percentage as ever is interested in it. You've got to remember there's a lot more folks nowadays.

"It would not do me to give advice. I'm not a trained teacher, understand. Don't claim to be. I just claim to be a student of the Book.

"But anybody who is asked to teach a Sunday School ought not to hesitate for a moment. The thing to remember is this: A man wants the truth.

"You'd be surprised how much people want to hear the truth."

Jammed Cars, Weak Stomachs, Suicides Routine For John LeMay

September 12, 1956

There MAY HAVE BEEN A TIME when an elevator operator could have gotten by knowing how to press a button and count up to 20. (In the case of the Empire State Building, up to 102, but let's keep it local).

Anyway, the day of the dumb elevator man is over. Take John LeMay of the Liberty Life Building, a mechanical-medical-psychological whiz.

If an elevator stops between floors—and it happens daily, John LeMay can unstick it. Or if not, he can summon another elevator, remove the side panels of both and transfer his passengers, bag and baggage.

If a citizen's stomach can't take the speed (16 seconds from top to bottom when the skids are well greased) John LeMay has a head full of first aid measures.

Another angle to his job is the trickiest of all. He's supposed to spot suicides before they jump.

"That's a problem all tall buildings have," he says. "Any time anybody gets on I don't know, I watch them carefully. Maybe I talk to them. If they look disturbed, or anything like that, I run the elevator slow and talk to them longer."

"Maybe I ask them where they're going. If they say they're going to a doctor's office, say, I wait and make sure they really go in.

"I think we've stopped some suicides that way. You're never really sure, but I think so."

None of the 800 people who work in the Liberty Life Building give their floor numbers to John LeMay. He knows them all.

And none of them are as proud of the building as he is. "It's like," he says, "a second home." From the top, he can point out the buildings of Concord and Mount Holly and the bump on the horizon that is King's Mountain.

It's not all glory, though, this modern elevator operating. There are problems, and the biggest problem is the door jumper.

"They come out of nowhere," John LeMay says. "You look both ways, you look up in the mirror and lean out and holler, 'Going Up!' and then when you close the door, like as not, somebody dives through it. You never know where they come from."

John LeMay has a favor to ask of elevator riders:

"Tell 'em not to do that.

"I caught a man's head in the door just a few weeks ago, and it really gave me a scare.

"Tell 'em to just let me know they're coming."

No Fame Nor Riches Came For Dan James—He Had Them

September 13, 1956

D AN JAMES NEVER SAW THE WORLD. Oh, he made little trips every now and then, but he was born within a block of the corner of Belmont Ave. and Harrill St. in the Belmont section; and last week, he died there.

So you couldn't say he was famous or rich or sophisticated. What you can say about Dan James is that he was a man.

He was a printer, and he would have made a better living at it than he did if he hadn't done so much of his printing without charge.

C.H. Farrar at the grocery store on the corner knows about that. "If anybody needed free work done," he says, "Dan never charged them. He couldn't do enough for the churches. If he saw he could help them, he was just one of those people who had to do it."

"If anybody was down on his luck," Mrs. Deason over at Deason's service station remembers, "Dan would always give them a dollar or two, whatever he could spare. He never had an enemy."

"I just never met a man like he was," another neighbor

said. "He'd play with the kids and give them things and he really enjoyed helping them out of their troubles. You couldn't count all the boys and girls he's helped out.

"And whenever anybody was sick around here, Mr. James would be there to sit up with them and see what he could do ... "

You see what kind of man he was. Not the kind you could write a story or make a movie about.

Just the kind you remember, for a lot of reasons, and you shed no tears when he is gone. Tears are for the empty lives of those who have made the world no better.

Around The World 80 Times Makes Luke Koontz Nervous

September 14, 1956

T HERE MAY BE A SAFER DRIVER than Luke Koontz somewhere around, but until he shows himself, we will have to remain impressed with the fact that Luke Koontz has driven two million miles without denting a fender.

Stretching the zeros out, that's 2,000,000 miles. That's more traveling than Johnny Appleseed, Richard Halliburton and John Foster Dulles ever chalked up among them. That's 80 times around the world, and he did it without an accident.

That establishes Luke Koontz, who pilots a Central Motor Lines tractor-trailer between Greensboro and Chicago, as a fugitive from the law of averages.

"It makes me a little nervous," he says.

If you looked at the statistics on this sort of thing, it would make you nervous, too. Luke should have driven into a telephone pole about a million miles back down the road.

Why hasn't he?

"I guess I'm what you'd call a real careful driver. I never take a chance, and I always try to think ahead so I'm ready for anything anybody else on the road happens to do."

When there's ice on the road, Luke Koontz drives as if every curve might be his last. When he's sleepy, he stops and sleeps. His cargo hits the loading docks as soon as the next guy's.

"Another thing that helps," he says, "is that I know everything is all right at home in Tyro (near Lexington). I don't have to worry. I don't have to think about anything but driving."

Worriers, Luke Koontz had observed, take a second or two longer to get their minds from their worries and their feet to the brakes—sometimes a second or two too long.

As 1954 Driver of the Year in North Carolina, as a winner of a golden cup from Gov. Hodges and a citation from Arthur Godfrey, as wearer of a "Master Driver" shoulder patch, Luke Koontz has had his share of honors.

He's had close calls, too. "I've had to go off the road a time or two," he says, "but I've managed to avoid an accident by just staying away from other vehicles. The best advice for a driver is 'Keep your distance.' They can't hit you if you're not there."

They ought to print that, in red ink, and paste it on a few million American windshields.

Star-Gazing Mrs. Kelly Lectures
To Starry-Eyed Young Audience

September 15, 1956

SAGITTARIUS, in case you are one of those who think it looks like an archer, really looks more like a teapot.

Argon, a gas which is inside light bulbs and hardly anywhere else on earth, is just all over the place on Mars.

And Mars, we would note in passing, is a mere 36 million miles away from Charlotte this week. You'll have to wait until 1971 to feel the same proximity again.

We picked up these gems of astral intelligence from Mrs. Luther W. Kelly the other afternoon while star-gazing under the inky 14-foot dome of the Children's Nature Museum planetarium.

Twice a week, more often by special request, Mrs. Kelly sits at the planetarium control panel, brings on midnight by turning a knob, and fills the "sky" with stars and planets. Then she tells the story of the universe to an audience of open-mouthed youngsters.

This is a fairly large order, calling for a poet as well as a scientist. Mrs. Kelly would deny being either, but she is both ...

"Mars," she told her listeners, "will be perfectly beautiful for the next two or three months."

She aimed an arrow of light to point out Mars.

"It's the nearest to earth of all planets," she said, "and it is an interesting planet with markings that seem to change colors with the season and polar caps that advance and recede ...

"Someday, scientists say, maybe within your lifetime, men will find out much more about Mars than they now know—and someday, undoubtedly, they will actually reach it."

The hum of the machine was the only sound in the room, as her listeners, caught up in the mystery of Mars, watched it disappear on the horizon.

"Venus is the morning star now," Mrs. Kelly went on. "I saw it the other morning, very, very early, passing beside a thin crescent of an old moon ...

"I felt I could almost touch it. It was a beautiful moment, but I had to get up early to see it. We miss many things like that. We sleep right through them."

Her voice, coming from the darkness with Venus rising in the east, somehow reminded her listeners that it had been a long time since they had looked to see if the stars were still there.

It suddenly seemed a good idea to walk away from the street lights that night to find a hilltop under the cold serenity of the Milky Way, and to seek out Sagittarius.

If you didn't find it, that would be all right.

This Here's A Wildcat, One Who Gets Tackled By Women

September 18, 1956

THE UNLIKELY FIGURE YOU SEE DANGLING AT RIGHT, the only such animal in or out of captivity who wears argyle socks, is perfectly harmless, unless you happen to be rooting against Central High School's football team.

His name is Welch Bostick Jr.

Age: 16.

Occupation: Wildcat.

The way he got to be a wildcat was they drafted Tex Berryhill. Tex was the wildcat, cavorting cut-up at halftime of Central games, for two or three years. Selective Service put a collar on him this year, and he passed down the long underwear dyed yellow, the cape with ears, the tennis shoes, to this wild kitten, Bostick.

What he didn't pass down was his tail. Some out-of-town

rooters tore it off for a victory souvenir last year. Welch will have his new tail shortly.

"I'm not as good a wildcat as Tex yet," Welch says. "I'm still learning."

Being a wildcat, after all, is not just the easiest thing in the world. You sort of grow into the job.

"It's mostly just keeping up the spirit at the pep rallies and games," Welch says. "We've got the team to have a great season if the school will just get behind it. I think we'll win at least seven."

Spoken like a snarler of bare fang and bold stripe, which, when he swings into action, Welch is.

"It's not easy, though," he insists. "You get hot as the dickens in that suit, for one thing. And the other side is always trying to get you.

"Like the Myers Park game. I went over to their side of the field and some of their girl cheerleaders jumped me. They grabbed me and threw me down and held on to me.

"It's not easy."

Sounds real tough.

They Gave His Dollar Back, With The GOC Sure Winner

September 19, 1956

ROCKINGHAM—His name is Robert T. Beaty, but they call him "Pop," and he's a dreamer.

He's also a loyal member of the Ground Observer Corps, that little band of sky watchers who help defend America.

And that's where the dream comes in.

Pop Beaty sort of figured he had done his part for his country. He furnished three sons to the service, didn't he? And when he was a young man in his native Scotland, he enlisted in the Army, didn't he? And fought the Hun in France, and Belgium?

Sure he did, he figured, so when he came to Rockingham to live, he gave an hour every now and then to the Ground Observer Corps and that was his share, he thought.

And then he had his dream. Let him tell you.

"I dreamed I died and went to heaven.

"When I knocked on the Pearly Gates, Saint Peter said, 'What do you want, Pop?'

"I says, 'I want to come in!'

"Saint Peter says, 'Well, what did you do when you were on earth?'

" 'Well,' I says, 'I put in six hours for the Rockingham Ground Observer Corps in good old Rockingham, N.C.'

"Saint Peter says, 'Come here, Pop. See yonder down there? That's Rockingham and do you see the lady down there? That's Mrs. Marge Meginnis. She has over 750 hours, and do you see that little broad fellow next to her?'

" 'Yeah,' I say.

" 'That's Mike, her husband. He has over 1,200 hours in. What other good deed do you think you have done on earth?'

"I says I gave a dollar to a blind man once.

"Then Saint Peter said, 'You put in six-hours in the Ground Observer Corps and you gave a blind man a dollar. Okay.'

"He calls to his right hand man and says, 'Gabriel, give Pop back his dollar and just let him go to Hell.' "

You can't keep Pop Beaty away from the binoculars.

Thus By Ox-Carts, Beer, Coeds, Will Freshmen Find The Truth

September 20, 1956

THE CREW CUT and the white buck shoes mark him. He is a freshman, and at the University of North Carolina, at State and Duke and Wake Forest, at Slippery Rock Teachers and Charlotte College, this is his week.

He goes into battle young, but not so young as he was last summer; ignorant as he looks to the sophomores; and confident, but not so confident as he tries to appear.

"What," Professor Horace Williams used to inquire of his UNC freshmen, "is the most important part of an ox-cart?"

He will wrestle with questions like that, questions with no relation, on the surface, to the real world of cars and football and fraternity parties. He will answer, the ox? The hitch? The wheels?

"Think about it," Professor Williams used to say. "I will tell you tomorrow."

So he will think about it, maybe the first time he ever thought about any philosophical question, and he will be a better man for it.

In the meantime, he will buy a pipe, write a letter home on stationery with the college seal up top and wash his socks for the first time in his life. He will drink his first beer, find it bitter and never, never admit it.

If he is lucky, he will have some great man like Robert Burton House, master of arts and doctor of laws, tell him, "Poetry is as practical as plowing—and plowing is as beautiful as poetry." He may think about that, too.

He will discover that teachers, even teachers, can be interesting people; that restaurant food, after the 150th time around, is not so glamorous; that the high school line doesn't work on the coeds, who have heard it all before; that football teams, by the nature of things, sometimes lose.

He will have his mind changed and his horizon broadened, and when he goes back for the answer to that ox-cart question, he will begin to understand what education is all about.

"The most important part of an ox-cart," Horace Williams used to his tell his freshmen, "is the idea."

At Two Or Three Per Second, Grandpop Would Have Swooned

September 21, 1956

FRANK SANTNER'S GRANDFATHER would have swooned dead away.

The old European brewmaster would have been proud of his grandson, understand, occupying the same job in a nice, modern place like the Atlantic brewery down on Graham St.

What would have knocked the old guy out are the huge bins of malt, the giant tanks of beer and ale, the bottles whipping through the capping machine at the rate of two per second.

Even the title has changed. Frank Santner isn't a brewmaster, he's the production manager.

This is Frank Santner, talking to you about his job.

"The two most important ingredients of beer are malt and water. The Charlotte water is almost perfect, we just harden it a very little. The malt comes from barley, the big, juicy kind of barley they grow in the Dakotas ... "

Down the stairs to the storage room.

"Chew on this malt. The nearer we can get the beer to taste like that, the better we like it. Then we ad corn grits, plain old corn grits, and hops. Hops is, I dunno, kind of like kudzu, a fast-growing vine. You press the flowers together and the center of the flowers, called 'lupulin,' gives the beer its bitterness ... "

Into the fermentation room.

"Here's where we add yeast. The beer ferments here for 14 days at 45 degrees. The ale fermentation room is a little warmer, and we use a different type yeast. That's the big difference between beer and ale, the kind of yeast. There are thousands of kinds and we could get thousands of flavors, if anybody would like them ... "

Into the aging room.

"The beer ages here for six to eight weeks. Then it's filtered and made brilliant, carbonated, and then run through this U.S. tax meter on the way to be bottled ... "

Into the bottling plant.

"The bottles are sterilized here, filled, capped, pasteurized, labels pasted on—all automatically—and then loaded into boxes automatically. Boxes run at two a second, cans at three a second. You can run cans faster because they don't break and you can pasteurize them faster too, because the metal conducts heat better.

"Okay?"

Okay, cheers and bottoms up.

But Grandpop never would have believed it.

With Digger Buried in Work, His Protege Left On His Own

September 24, 1956

W HAT DOES A FLAGPOLE SIT-
TER DO when people tire of
flagpole sitting?

"Only one thing to do,"
John Pappas says. "Go under-
ground."

So John Pappas changed
his billing from "The Human
Bird" to "The Human Corpse"
and marched out to seek his
fortune six feet under.

"I became," he says, without a note of pride, "a student
of Digger O'Dell."

Digger O'Dell, in case you didn't know it, is just the
holder of the world title for being buried alive—57 days in
Atlanta, Ga., for which he received a cool 18 grand and forgot
how to use his legs. He was out at—rather, under Airport Park
a few years back.

Anyway, John Pappas is in town, staying at the Belmont
Hotel, well above ground, and looking for a job at the

Southern States Fair this week.

He parted company with Digger on the banks of the Potomac just last week.

"Me and Digger had a little disagreement," he says. "I was supposed to be buried on the Maryland side and him on the Virginia side. Well, he got down there and forgot all about me. So I left him.

"There wasn't," he suggested as an afterthought, "much old Digger could do about it."

The Fair week job—if he finds it—will be John's eighth trip under. His personal record is 17 days in Huntington, W. Va.

"Easiest job I ever had," he claims. "You get down there, see, with plenty of food and a radio and maybe a telephone. You're lying in a coffin packing case, see, not a coffin, and you've got plenty of room to roll around. There's a hole up to the surface to breathe through and let people see you and talk to you, and maybe a telephone."

What does a human corpse do to pass the time?

"Mostly pray it don't rain," John Pappas says. "If it rains, you're going to get water seepage, and if it rains hard, you're going to get wet, and it rains real hard, you're liable to wake up floating some night.

"It's a fair weather racket, all right. But these days—what isn't?"

To Head Chain Of Command,
Susan Had To Start With 'Z'

September 25, 1956

SUCCESS FOR SUSAN REED, was just a matter of inflection.

That's the story, anyway, and it's straight out of a soap opera scenario. Can a chubby redhead from South Carolina find happiness as the toast of New York and West Coast cafe society?

The answer, of course, is "yes." But back there in 1946, when she first stepped before a night club audience in New York, Susan had her doubts.

She figured she better clue 'em in, so the first thing she said was, "This is a zither."

They laughed. They practically rolled in the aisles. They hardly listened to her folk songs at all.

Susan still had a hunch folk songs would go over with those cider-sipping sophisticates, but she had to upgrade her act.

So she threw in a haughty pause in her introduction. She didn't smile at her audience when she came out. She looked them straight in the eye and said, "This—is a zither."

They stopped talking. They sat there open-mouthed. This—is a zither? Wow!

Having established her command of the big city night-clubbers, however, Susan reverted to her chubby redheaded self. She went to running an antique shop in Greenwich Village and turning her Palmetto charm on her neighbors.

Sunday, she came back to Carolina's sunny clime and crooned folk songs to the folks at the Mint Museum.

She showed flashes of urbanity, all right.

"I never could sing as loud as Gladys Swarthout, but Miss Swarthout can't play the zither.

"Elvis Presley? I think he really ought to MARRY that microphone."

But the tipoff came when she introduced herself. She gave it out straight.

"This is a zither."

She was among friends.

Pupil Flipped, So Teacher Stays Tanked With Starlet

September 26, 1956

W ILLIAM BLAKE IS PROBABLY the only graduate of Harding High School who ever made a porpoise ring a schoolbell, shoot basketballs through a net, sing, raise a flag, leap 25 feet out of the water, play catch with a football, jump through a hoop, pull a dog named Fifi through the water on a surfboard and shake hands.

Don't you reckon?

He does all of this at Marineland in Florida. Or rather, Splash, Algae and Flippy II do it, to the amusement of 100,000 people every year, and William Blake teaches them.

Just now, Splash and Algae are the stars of the show. William's big job is to bring Flippy II (Flippy I, the world's first poised porpoise, flipped right out of the tank not long ago and died of internal injuries) along to stardom.

Flippy II was captured a few months ago.

"You can't catch 'em with a net," William warns. "They'll drown. We fire a clamp at their tails. It grabs them without hurting them. They learn fast. They're almost as smart as chimpanzees, but not quite, and, by the way, all that stuff about porpoises saving drowning people is nonsense, even if it DID happen to Little Orphan Annie the other day.

"But you teach 'em things very easily just by giving 'em plenty of fish when they do it right. People just can't get over Algae shooting baskets with a basketball. He rarely misses. Algae's the high jumper, too. Twenty-five feet out of the water. He starts at the very bottom and comes roaring out of there.

"You know, a porpoise is a mammal. He can live on dry land if he stays wet, but he likes the water better. We keep the water at 68 degrees in the Wintertime to keep 'em from catching cold."

Porpoises are the funniest people since monkeys.

But don't laugh.

Can YOU pull a dog named Fifi through the water on a surfboard?

It Was A Gallant Effort But It Was No Good Day To Try

September 27, 1956

W ET STREETS WERE NOT THE SOLE HERITAGE of the storm.

There was, for example, the newsboy.

He strained toward the Square through the whipping rain, his mop of blond hair dripping water, his tweed coat soaked, his papers wrapped in an old plastic bag and dry.

On his way down W. Trade St., the boy stopped under an awning to make sure the corners were all tucked in. He crowded beside the people waiting for buses, and they moved aside to avoid getting wetter than they already were.

When he finally made it to the jewelry store, he walked into the doorway, shook himself like a pooch climbing out of a duck pond, and examined the papers again.

Still dry.

The rain swept across the Square in sheets. He looked at it, wondering what to do. You can't sell papers in a doorway, and you can't sell papers in the rain, either.

He finally got as close as he could to the square column supporting the jewelry store roof, put his papers down carefully on a box and sat on another one. Gusts of rain splattered the plastic bag covering the papers.

A tall man with a black umbrella stopped, dug in his pocket for a nickel and the boy reached gingerly under the bag and gave him a paper. The rain left big splotches of water on the next paper down.

The boy looked as if he were thinking:

"If somebody would give me a quarter, I would give him the whole bundle and go home."

It was five minutes before the next customer bothered to stop in the rain to buy a newspaper.

The newsboy lifted the cover quickly, but not quickly enough. The wind caught the two top papers and blew them into the sidewalk. The next gust lifted them, pages flying into Tryon St.

"Look at that," the newsboy said to nobody. "Look at that. Aw ... "

He handed the man his paper and sat back down on the wet box, and it was hard to tell from looking at his face where the rain stopped and the tears began.

Bob Prospers As Flame Dies, And Cat Resembles Guinea Pig

September 28, 1956

B OB RAIFORD, WHO BROKE THE RULES on his WBT disc jockey show a few months ago and got fired for it, has found a home.

He's interviewing celebrities and playing records from the Cafe Rouge of the Statler in New York. And if he gets ordered off the air now, it'll be coast-to-coast, because he working for NBC (WSOC, 2:30 p.m. daily.)

A letter from Martha Farmer, the Norfolk, Va., girl who found love in the Charlotte bus station and used PEOPLE to find her lover. The thrill is gone, the flame is dead, and Martha's ringless fingers are back on the old stand—typing letters for a Norfolk business firm.

We are happy to report that John Pappas has found employment. You'll be able to visit him at the Southern States Fair. But you'll have to look down. His job—"the easiest in the world"—is burying himself six feet under for the edification and amusement of passersby.

Remember Arnold L. Hill, the ex-airman who has saved a bottle of Coca-Cola—unopened—since 1942, just in case he ever gets thirsty? Well, he's still got a cap on it, and next month's issue of the national Coca-Cola magazine will feature Mr. Hill and the 14-year-old Pause the Refreshes.

A couple of months ago, PEOPLE told the story of a little girl who wanted to buy a $7.95 doll and couldn't understand that 18 cents wasn't enough.

A lot of folks with the $7.77 to spare called in, and one lady said, "I have a $40 doll my daughter doesn't want any more. Do you think the Salvation Army could use it?"

Some remark, sure, would have been appropriate at that moment, but we couldn't think of it, and we still can't.

Welch Bostick, the Central Wildcat, made a tail for his costume one afternoon ... and it got ripped off at a football game that night ... and Central lost. Even among wildcats, there's no justice.

And then there was Jimmy Blackmon, the rocket builder, a PEOPLE of early August.

Well, you know about Jimmy.

October 1956

———

There was no reason other than here's a story to tell. It's not here's a story to tell because this person has an impact here. We have a lot of good writers in the country, but I don't read very many pieces in magazines and newspapers about so-called nobodies, and he took people who would be considered nobodies, and made them somebodies. It was not, you should know about this person because—it was just you should know about this person because you passed him on the street and he has got an interesting story to tell, he's in our midst, he's part of the fabric of our lives, and if you don't know about it, here's an interesting story I want to tell you about him.

—Julian Scheer, reporter, *Charlotte News*

Off Into The Sunset They Ride, But On Alert For Filter Traps

October 1, 1956

O NE OF THESE DAYS we are going to wake up in this country and find that the Western movie has ridden down the long trail to oblivion and we will all be the worse for it.

You couldn't have pawned off this proposition five years ago when every B-movie house in the nation was thriving on the double feature and Hopalong Cassidy was just beginning to gallop across the picture tubes.

But things have changed.

If you had been standing in front of Tryon Theater Saturday afternoon, you'd have gotten the point. The kids were there, as always. The popcorn smell wafted out on to Tryon St., as always. But the double feature had capitulated to the quadruple feature and the nearest thing to a Western in all that jungle of celluloid starred Victor Mature.

Victor Mature. The kids stacked up their bikes on the sidewalk to see Victor Mature in buckskin. There is something vaguely obscene about this.

Time was when Saturday afternoons could be reduced to a simple formula: Smiley Burnette was to Gene Autry as Gabby Hayes was to Roy Rogers.

Even these cowboys, who were given to breaking into song at crucial places in their films, were considered a little too esoteric by us pimply-faced devotees to Tom Mix, Buck Jones and Wild Bill Elliott.

The scenarios were clean, firm and flawless. The good guys wore white hats and never fooled around with women and could outdraw the bad guys with their backs turned.

What has come of the sagebrush and stagecoach strong men today?

Well, last year was the year Gene Autry, with maybe a couple of sarsaparillas too many, fell off his horse at a Fort Worth rodeo and Don (Red) Harris was found smooching Susan Hayward by an angry girl friend. Just last week, they lassoed Lash LaRue on a stolen property count. And nearly every night that passes you can see Bill Elliott, wild no more, dolled in a fancy suit with Ivy League tie and the clasp selling Viceroy cigarettes on Channel 3. Ten thousand howling redskins to 10,000 filter traps in one change of costume.

Saturday's kids at the Tryon quadruple feature were a new breed. One of them had a holster on his hip, but it had a ray gun in it.

So He Told Them, 'Bobby Lane,' And Then They Were Certain

October 2, 1956

KENNETH HEATH HAS A HARD TIME convincing people he's Bobby Lane. They think he's Elvis Presley.

Like the other evening at Park Center. Kenneth (that's what his mama named him) climbed between the ropes to manipulate the sponge and water bottle in the corner of one Jimmy Carter.

"Elvis!" hollered an eagle-eyed teen-aged ringsider.

A dozen others got the point immediately.

"Elvis!" they screamed.

For Kenneth, busy at being Bobby Lane, who he is when he's fighting and seconding, it was a little disconcerting. He has the long sideburns, the disinterested mouth, the nose (slightly battered from 66 wins, six losses and two draws, but still Presleyan) and the casual manner, but Kenneth Heath would like for one and all to know he is a middleweight named Bobby Lane, not a sideshow freak.

"I mean," he explained later in the presence of his manager Honest Jawn Allen, "you can't get nobody to take you sirrusly if these teenagers act like that all the time."

"And this boy is a good fighter, too," Mr. Allen said.

"Like down in Miami, where I'm training now," Bobby said.

"Yeah, training with Dykes, Kilgore, all those fellers," Mr. Allen said.

"Well, down there I drive a courtesy car for an Oldsmobile dealer," Bobby said, "and when I go, I go right sharped up, see."

"He's doing fine down there, winning every fight. He's got a real punch and they're noticing him," Mr. Allen said.

"Well, anyway, one time all these girls hollered 'Elvis' and came running and got in the car. What could I do? They wouldn't believe I wasn't Elvis. They tore my coat. When they asked who I was if I wasn't Elvis. I told 'em Kenneth Heath. They didn't believe me, so I told 'em Bobby Lane. Then they were SURE I was Elvis."

"Don't confuse him," Mr. Allen said. "He's really Bobby Lane ... "

"I can't get in the ring without somebody hollering 'Elvis.' "

"Elvis managed by Honest Jawn Allen," Mr. Allen said.

And he never touched a git-tar in his life.

Newspaper Office A Bold Mine
For Fred Friend, Collector

October 3, 1956

THIS IS FRED FRIEND, who collects.

Fred Friend is nine years old, goes to O'Donoghue School, lives on Poindexter Circle, and collects.

Newspaper offices being veritable gold mines for the undiscriminating collector, Fred Friend can often be found in this one.

This is an unretouched manuscript of Fred Friend engaged in collecting:

"Hi. Do you have any sports pictures or airplane pictures or anything like that? I collect things. I try to lay 'em away in a chest or something like that. If I could have that picture of Elvis Presley, I'd put it in a nice place or sell it to some of the girls. We live near a high school. I collect almost anything. I like to pick up various stones and things like that. I don't have a very big room but most of the time I just throw 'em in the basement. My mother doesn't like it too much. She's always kidding me and she throws a lot of them away. I found some money one time. I didn't know what a centipede was the first time I saw one but I didn't pick it up. They're poisonous. Once I found a bird and hid him under a tree and when I came back there was a big old snake and no bird. That's a pretty calendar. Maybe when it gets January I'll be up to get a picture. I like that. I read the *National Geographic* magazine. I have a friend who lives near me. He just collects postcards."

Period. New paragraph.

"Well, goodbye."

We don't know what his mama will think, but Fred Friend went out loaded down with old photos.

Including sports picture and airplane pictures and things like that.

Thirty Years Ago, Sun Beamed On Big Fight Of The Carolinas

October 4, 1956

T HE OLD GUY WITH THE BEARD and the dog on a leash walked through the crowds of people, past the throaty sideshow barker, past the laughter of the ferris wheel, past the kids throwing baseballs at bottles.

There seemed to be no particular reason for his presence at the fair. He walked with his head down, not even looking around as if he had seen it all before, as if it were part of his daily life, new and live and thrilling no more.

His name, he said, was Lew Carpenter. He had a nervous disorder of some sort and his arms jerked when he talked.

"There are people," he said, "who remember me."

His eyes swept the pressing, noisy crowd of people. He didn't find anyone who remembered him there.

"I used to fight," he said. "I traveled with carnivals and circuses, meeting all comers."

He stopped to think.

"It was right here in 19 ... Nineteen and twenty-six, I think," he said, "when I fought Terry Roberts for the middle-weight championship of the Carolinas. March, 1926."

The dog strained at the leash.

"This is cowboy," the man said. "He's the dog who bit a man out here last year. The man stepped on his foot. Maybe you remember that. Cowboy would not have bit that man if he hadn't stepped on his foot."

The crowd jostled around Lew Carpenter. He backed against a tent flap to talk.

"I've been in show business, off and on, all my life," he said. "I'm growing tired of it now ... "

His voice trailed off.

"In fact," he said, "the only reason I'm out here at all today is because of Cowboy."

He produced a tiny clown hat and put it on the dog's head.

"It's a funny thing, but Cowboy likes fairs and circuses. Seems like he's happiest when he's at a place like this. He can walk on his hind legs and hold a pipe in his teeth. And the fair is just the place he's got to be."

That's why he was there. Because of Cowboy. It had been a long time since the people crowded around the boxing ring under the sun to watch Lew Carpenter take on all comers.

Nobody cared about Lew Carpenter any more.

But Cowboy could walk on his hind legs and hold a pipe in his teeth. The people still clapped for Cowboy.

Tourist Sam Has Jaundiced Eye After Long Look At Charlotte

October 5, 1956

P ARDON ME BUDDY," the voice said.

It was a monkey sitting on a parking meter.

"Yes?" we inquired. (After that crazy elephant stomping around in the western suburbs this time last year, after journalistic encounters with a steer on the Pearl St. playground, a heron in Myers Park and thousands of dead fish at Freedom Park, no mere talking monkey on a Tryon St. parking meter was going to faze us.)

"Can you spare a nickel?" the monkey asked.

"A nickel?" we asked.

"A nickel," the monkey said.

We decided to make the step. "For a cup of coffee?" we asked.

"For the meter, stupid," the monkey said. "I have already had one run-in with the cops in this town and I do not want another. I need to feed this one-armed bandit."

"Here you are, Mac," we said.

"The name is Sam," the monkey said, shoving the coin into the slot and turning the crank. "I am passing through from Brooklyn."

He sat back on his haunches and surveyed the street haughtily.

"What kind of hick town are you running here anyway?" he chattered. "I am visiting a friend out on Belgrave Pl. the other afternoon and I climb a tree just for the exercise. Right away everybody gets excited. I cross this Morehead, or whatever it is, and spend the night in a sycamore on Greenwood Cliff. Along about dawn, some guy from the Pet Dept. clamps a net over my had. What kind of way is that to treat tourists?"

"Oh," we ventured, "it's not such a bad town … "

"Yeah?" Sam said. "You got a ball team?"

"The Charlotte Hornets," we said proudly.

"And I supposed they finished in the second division?" Sam asked.

"They finished second," we said, "and if the Cards hadn't tripped Milwaukee up like that… "

"If me no ifs," Sam said. "I am sitting here patiently waiting for my owner and companion to come out of that building where he is dickering with somebody to move our pet shop from Brooklyn to this corn-pone town, and Lord knows why, in order that I may go back to Ebbet's Field for the windup."

"Look," we said, unable to stand it any longer, "how does it happen that you are able to carry on intelligent, if antagonistic, conversation? How do you talk?"

"Stop asking stupid questions," Sam said. "Everybody in Flatbush can talk about baseball."

He leaned over confidentially.

"You want a good tip?" he asked. "It can't miss.

"The Dodgers in six."

Everybody Has Been In Hurry, So 'Guv' Comes Out 'Aszheo'

October 8, 1956

THIS BEING THE TIME OF THE BANDWAGON, the red, white and blue All-American season of posters, the dancing girls, the bunting draped platform, the megaphone, the Tele-prompter, the sincere promise, the toothy smile and the firm handshake, this being the year of the New America and the Great Crusade (Chapter Two), we decided to see what is up among the polls.

Polly Hershberger, whom we had never met, gave us a large Democratic hello from behind her desk at 6th and Tryon.

"Golly," she said, "things are going fine. We had a wonderful opening with the Governor and everybody here. Would you sign the guest book, please? I've got to get rid of this Coke bottle. Democrats are always leaving things around here. Thomas M. Fairbanks was the first one to sign the book. Kerr Scott and Hodges are in there too."

"Who," we asked, "is Lutton A. Aszheo?"

"That's Luther H. Hodges," Mrs. Hershberger said. "He was in a hurry. We've all been in a hurry around here. The Republicans have their material out already, but we think a lot of it will get rain-soaked and just melt away before November. We're working through the precinct chairman. The Young Democrats are staffing the office. We are open every day from 9 to 5, Saturdays too. There are two back rooms, one for typing and mailing and one for conferences. Did you see the piece in *Colliers* about Stevenson's sons? It was fine, but we're not very happy about the Norman Rockwell painting for the cover of *Saturday Evening Post*. Mrs. Scott Summers is doing a really wonderful job for us, and Mrs. Gatling too. And people are coming by, oh, my goodness! We've never had so many people wanting to work as this year. I think Stevenson really has a good chance, don't you? This Hugh Haynie cartoon about the Republicans being scared, I like. I'm going to leave it on the bulletin board all through the campaign. *The New York Times* is running the full text of the speeches of both Stevenson and Eisenhower. I don't see how anybody could vote Republican if they would just read those speeches. Have a Douglas button, won't you? Do you know I haven't had a chance to eat any lunch yet? We really need more than one phone."

We thanked Mrs. Hershberger and walked out past the red, white and blue crepe paper and a vase filled with daisies and American flags. She was already back at work, with Jack Love peering over her shoulder from the wall, and we went down to see the GOP, about which we'll tell you tomorrow.

Between Henry And Rhinestones, Somebody's Gonna Win Election

October 9, 1956

FOR ALL WE KNOW, Henry Krajewski of Secaucus, N.J. is going to be elected president. Henry certainly wants to be president. He is running under the banner of Poor Man's Party up there in New Jersey and has swayed a number of patrons in his Secaucus tavern, two or three, we understand, while they were cold sober.

The point we are trying to make is that while yesterday we interviewed Polly Hershberger of the Mecklenburg Democrats and while today we are about to quote Emma Hinson of the Republicans, we stand absolutely ready to grant equal time to Henry Krajewski and to the Independent Electors of South Carolina, the American Constitution Party of Iowa, the Prohibition Party, Socialist Labor party, Socialist Workers Party, Socialist Party, States Rights Party of Louisiana, Kentucky States Rights Party, Constitution Party of Tennessee, Conservative Party of New Jersey, Texas Constitution Party, Mississippi Republican Party, Black and Tan GOP Party and the Independent Presidential Electors of Alabama. That is how confused things are in a Presidential voting year.

Mrs. Emma H. Hinson, GOP office secretary, is more worried about Adlai Stevenson than Henry Krajewski, but seems hardly worried about either.

"Things are just fine," she said. "If you don't think there are a lot of Republicans around here, you just ought to try to contact every one of them, as we're trying to do. We're getting a lot of help, of course. Jonas has his own office and the State Republican headquarters and the Citizens for Eisenhower are very busy here. I've had close to 100 volunteers to work for us. Nobody is getting paid, either. We have some wonderful candidates. The biggest thing we have to fight, I suppose, is the fact, no, call it an 'impression' that people can't have a say-so in their local elections if they don't register Democratic. Now, that's defeatist thinking, of course. And then we're having to tell people over and over that they must not mark the straight Democratic circle if they want to split their ballot. That worries us a little. Mecklenburg is getting to be a big metropolitan center, now, and a lot of native Republicans are coming in from up North. I was converted in '52, myself. First, you have to get interested in politics and after that you become a Republican. We had an old man come in here the other day and say he was voting Democratic because he never had it so good. Can you imagine? After four years of a Republican administration he never had it so good and THAT'S why he's voting Democratic ... "

Mrs. Hinson had to scoot out the door at that point to catch a fetching Republican lady who had dropped her gloves. So we put out a cigarette in an Ike ashtray, walked past a display of Ike earrings, Ike hosiery, Ike tie clasps and rhinestone elephants, and left.

And In The Night, Talent Came, To Leave His Calling Card

October 10, 1956

W HEN THE SUN CAME UP, the sign was hanging just as you see it at right, as if it belonged there. Whether mute testimony to some young man's personal experience, a carefully conceived plot or an innocent spur-of-the-moment prank, we cannot tell you and wouldn't if we could. The sign was down by nine o'clock in the morning, but it had served its eloquent purpose admirably.

The Queens sign proves for perhaps the millionth time that people are never so inspired as when engaged in skullduggery. We have no patience with those who drop bags full of water on citizens from hotel rooms or pull chairs from under fat dowagers or fill a sleeping man's mouth with shaving cream, understand. They called in Pinkertons when some lads who shall be nameless flushed small quantities of TNT into the innards of the Central High School plumbing system several years ago, and that is all right and proper.

But there is plenty of evidence that William Shakespeare,

Abraham Lincoln, Lord Halifax and Uncle Remus would have chuckled at the Queens sign, and indeed, given half a chance, might have hung it up themselves.

That is the way with the famous. Calvin Coolidge used to hide in the in the White House bushes to frighten guards.

It was Jim Moran who hit upon the device of tying a piece of string around one ear and pulling the other end in his mouth. People were too polite to ask why.

And it was a well known publicity man named Al Horwits, according to legend, who invented the telegram which a hopeful Hollywood star receives occasionally.

DISREGARD MY PREVIOUS WIRE (SIGNED) ZANUCK

One of the finest, quietest, most successful pranks in history was pulled by a British *bon vivant* named Cole, who, after purchasing a ball of twine one day, ran into a well-dressed old gentleman he couldn't pass by.

"Look here," said Cole, "we are engaged in a bit of engineering on this corner and my assistant is at lunch. Would you mind holding the end of this string? Stand where you are and hold it tightly. We will be finished in a moment."

The elegant old guy obliged. Cole back away from him, reeling out the string down the sidewalk and around the corner. There Cole waited for a second gentleman, approached him in the same manner, cautioned him to stand firm and hold tight, and disappeared.

Cole could have stuck around to watch (considering the stability of the English) for an hour. But he didn't, according to H. Allen Smith, whose story this is. The warm glow of achievement for the imaginative prankster comes with the means, not the end.

The same thing is true of the Queens College sign hanger. We do not know who he is, but he has what it takes and if he applies himself will go far.

Old Man Sat, Stared Until A Child Happened To Pass

October 11, 1956

IT WAS FIVE O'CLOCK IN THE AFTER-NOON, that was part of the reason.

The elegant lady in the fur cape, the four businessmen and the two young housewives stood at the Tryon St. bus stop with the vacant look of people thinking about their own affairs, tired of working, tired of shopping and eager to get home.

So they didn't notice the old guy in the alley.

He wasn't much to notice. He sprawled against a brick wall and raised his stubble-covered face to the people who passed by and lifted a shaking arm to offer them a pencil.

Some stared at him curiously. Nobody stopped.

The people waiting for the bus didn't even look his way. The lady in fur stepped out to the curb impatiently and looked up the street to see if the bus was coming.

One of the four businessmen leaned against a plate glass window, took a newspaper from under his arm and turned to the sports page.

One of the housewives glanced uncomfortably at the old man in the alley, and looked away. They all waited.

That was when the little girl walked up. She was a few steps ahead of her mother, whose arms were full of packages. The little girl walked straight up to the old man in the alley and looked at him. He looked back. The little girl's mother took her place with the others, shifted the packages in her arms and began waiting for the bus.

"Come here, Annie," she said.

The little girl walked over.

"He's selling pencils," her mother said.

The man with the newspaper stared over at the little girl.

The little girl walked back over to the alley and peered down at the man.

She didn't say anything and neither did he.

She turned back to her mother and tugged at her arm.

"I want a pencil," she said.

Her mother smiled, took her pocketbook from her arm and reached into it awkwardly, without putting down the bulky packages. She gave the little girl a nickel.

The girl took it over to the ally and put it in the man's hat. She looked at him once more, then walked quietly back to her mother's side.

"God bless you," the old man mumbled. She didn't hear him.

The bus arrived and its doors opened.

Everybody got on.

But before they did, two of the businessmen and the lady with the furs dropped coins in the old guy's hat.

A little child had led them.

Despite Yale Or Record Player
The Breed Continues The Game

October 12, 1956

P EOPLE ARE A DREAMING BREED, full of hope and expectation.

You can see it in a youngster's face, lighted by the gaudy bulbs of the ferris wheel at an amusement park. You can read it between the furrowed brows of a weekend gambler trying to figure out whether Michigan State is 26 points better than Indiana and thinking six picks are worth 25 bucks.

The youngster will ride the ferris wheel and find it's really more exciting from the ground. The gambler will go with Michigan State but Rice or Yale or Texas A&M will trip him up. He won't win his 25 dollars; he hasn't yet. But he can dream.

Everybody does. The parents of one Charlotte youngster are dreaming of such a thing as a 33 rpm record player, even an old one, on which their son can listen to records of Mother Goose rhymes, of Robert Louis Stevenson poems, of all the stories and poems every child ought to know. He can't read them for himself because he is blind.

They may never have a record player for their son.

But they can dream.

Dreams do not have to be poignant. They can be pointless. They can be vacant, or sad, or frightening.

U.S. census figures list one man employed in Charlotte as a longshoreman. We do not know him, but he must be an interesting man—with a dream of the docks that are someplace else, not here.

In the course of a day, you can spot other dreamers. They crane their necks on a bus passing the law building to look up to the floor from which a man jumped to his death. And they are all putting themselves in his place and wondering—why?

In a 6th St. cafe, two men talk aimlessly of the fact that there are tunnels under the city streets, hollow remnants of the day when gold was mined in Mecklenburg. They lapse into silence and their dreams carry them back. They are both digging, and both hitting a shimmering vein ...

People are a dreaming breed. You can see it in a letter to the editor written in pencil.

"I am a 11-year-old boy," it says, "who wish to help my Daddy. He or Mother don't know it but I see them cry about not being able to meet the bills ...

"I remember a story on TV one night about a little boy what wrote a letter to a newspaper man and he got lots of things. My Daddy is good to us all ... I'll pay the money back ... "

It is a touching letter and the only trouble is it is not in the handwriting of an 11-year-old boy at all, but in the handwriting of a woman ... of 35 or 40 perhaps, and that makes the letter somehow sadder.

People are a dreaming breed. And if things don't work out for people on the city streets as well as they do on Channel 3, all is not up with them.

They can still dream.

It'll Take A Man Named 'E.J.' For The Watch To Be A Sale

October 15, 1956

H E STOOD ON THE CURB BEFORE THE ROW OF PAWN SHOPS, cafes and clothing stores on the E. Trade St. hill. He lit a cigarette, tore the top of the pack to make sure it was his last one and threw the package away. He looked down at the crumpled package in the gutter as if it were interesting.

"Are you sure you don't want to buy it?" he asked.

He was an old man and his glasses made his eyes bulge when he looked up.

"Look, this ain't no cheap watch," he said. "It was made in Switzerland. My brother-in-law give it to me years ago and it ain't never missed a tick. I wouldn't think about selling it, but ... "

He reached in his pocket and took it out again.

"I need the money," he said.

He turned it over and over in his hand.

"I know not many people carry pocket watches any more," he said. "But I ain't one of these guys who goes around selling cheap stuff."

The sun caught the shiny gold back of the watch and flashed from it.

"I went to that damn place," he said.

He nodded at one of the pawn shops and spat in the gutter.

"That damn guy said he'd gimme three bucks and a half. He knew I needed the money, see. I told him I'd just sell it. Now—I don't know."

He held it by its old leather thong and looked at it.

"Maybe if you ain't interested I'll just hang on to the damn thing," he said. "To tell you the truth, it's the last thing I got that's worth having."

He opened the back and looked at the mechanism.

"I don't reckon your initials are 'E.J.' anyway, are they?" he asked. "Well that's what's carved in there. 'With best wishes to E.J.—Lonnie'

"I guess I'll have to find some guy named E.J., huh? That's just rich as hell, ain't it?"

He snapped the back shut and walked off down the hill, past the pawn shops, past two watch repair places and under the railroad track, with no money, no buyer and no prospect, and with the last thing he had that was worth having still in his pocket.

All That's Left These Days Can Run In Drugstore Window

October 16, 1956

T HE LITTLE SHOW WINDOW OF ECKERD'S on N. Tryon St. nearly stopped pedestrian traffic the other afternoon. It had no thousand-dollar display, either. What it did have was an electric train.

"Choo choo," a young-ster said.

"Train," his older sister corrected him. They both stayed to watch.

A boy pressed his nose against the glass and

stooped down so that the tiny spotlight of the engine came straight at him, then veered away just as it approached his face.

Another boy tugged at his father's sleeve. The two of them stopped, the youngster standing on tiptoes to look up at the train, the father stooping to look down at it.

The little boy said nothing. He just stared.

"That's an electric train, Jackie," his father said. "Would you like to have one someday?"

Jackie's eyes followed the train around and around the tiny track. "Uh-huh," he said.

The two walked away, Jackie looking back at the train.

In the space of half an hour, fully 100 youngsters and their parents were drawn to the window to put their fingers on it and watch the engine pulling a coal car, a flat-car, a box-car and a caboose in a tight circle.

There was a time when they could have gone down to the station and watched the real thing, a smoke-belching monster with a clanging bell and a hissing steam pipe.

That day is gone, of course. The steam engine is something they're putting in museums already, and the wail that youngsters hear far off in the night is not a steam engine but a diesel horn.

"Choo choo" is not even apt any longer, and the next generation of boys and girls will not use that childish term because that's not how trains sound today.

You couldn't have convinced the youngsters pressing their faces against Eckerd's window that there was ever anything finer than a sleek electric train going in a circle.

But their fathers knew—their fathers who have sat on a hillside and seen the smoke far around the bend and heard the incomparable, distant sound of a locomotive climbing a grade and waved to the fireman, a man with a gritty neckerchief. Their fathers knew better.

Things Are Calmer Since Days When Issues Brought Torn Shirts

October 17, 1956

I F THERE IS A FINER CLEARING HOUSE of humankind in this town than the Mecklenburg County Courthouse, it does not come to mind.

Johnny Goodrum knows. Most of the lawyers and land owners, bill payers, murderers, judges and politicians who have walked those marble corridors in the past 27 years have come under the observation of Johnny Goodrum, and he can tell you a thing or two about them.

"I expect it was over 20 years ago when Charlie Thornburg and Henry Fowler tore each other's shirts off in a County Commission meeting," he'll say.

"I don't remember what the issue was, but they felt right strong about it. They had to go home and get new shirts ... "

' Those were brave days in the Courthouse, but Johnny Goodrum, window washer, exofficio jailer and friend of all, claims these quiet days are better.

"Sid McAden, for example—now, he's the best Commission chairman we've ever had down here."

Even if he has never yet de-shirted his opponent.

"The jail has given us some interesting times. We had a

fellow run just last Saturday.

"But nobody's ever like one fellow we had. He had took off from the courtroom and I've never seen a man run so fast. He came down the stairs just when Query Alexander was coming up. Knocked him 20 feet.

"That fellow ran right down the hall and everybody he passed took out after him. He ran off the bank back of the Courthouse, jumped right into the middle of the street and disappeared. That one was gone for two months."

Johnny Goodrum just clears his throat and keeps on going. "It calmed down a good deal after the state took over the chain gangs from the county. I remember the time we had 100 prisoners upstairs. I used to lay down mattresses for them all to sleep on at night.

"Another thing we used to do is pour illegal liquor down the drain back of the building.

"Sometimes there'd be hundreds of gallons piled up in the back room. And every time they broke it up and poured it out, they had to send two city policemen down to the creek.

"If they didn't, why, there'd be people down there with buckets to catch that liquor, muddy water and all."

Johnny Goodrum grins to remember it.

"They used to say muddy water didn't hurt it much, but I wouldn't know about that."

Like A Feather Storm, Birds Flutter Down To Mrs. Shiver

October 18, 1956

T HERE IS AN OASIS OF KINDNESS AND HUMANITY in the indifferent heart of the hurrying city every afternoon at 4:30.

That is when Mrs. T.R. Shiver feeds the pigeons.

She walks under from the Tryon Theater marquee with a cupful of popcorn and the pigeons flutter down from their eaves, from their makeshift lofts among the rooftops, from their perches amid columns and gargoyles, from every direction.

They come by the score and stand on the curb facing her like dutiful children. After the first cup hits the pavement, they scratch and peck and pile up atop one another like frightened chickens, and Mrs. Shiver pours cup after cup in their midst.

"I think they've come to expect it," she says. "They used to hesitate, but now they're ready every day.

"They're the same ones, too. They sort of have their own personalities. There's Peg Leg over there. He only has one leg but he gets around all right. He always gets his share."

The daily ritual is always witnessed by a passerby or two who stops to watch the pigeons group on the spot.

"Every now and then," Mrs. Shiver says, "a certain man comes by. The pigeons jump to his hand when he wiggles a finger at them. He never feeds them, but they seem to know him—they certainly know him better than they do me. I can tell he talks to them right often.

"And I'm not the only one who feeds them, by the way. There are several people on Tryon St. who do it. The jeweler right up the street feeds them almost every day.

"If you watch them you can get to know them pretty well. There are some who seem to lead the others, and some who have a hard time getting food, just like it is in the human world," I suppose.

The feeding takes five or 10 minutes. Then Mrs. Shiver goes back to work inside the theater.

The human world rushes into the tiny oasis and the last pigeon strutting about looking for spare kernels flies away, back to his airy haunts above the streets.

Wednesday Was Such A Day When He'd Be Out Despite It

October 19, 1956

W EDNESDAY'S WIND caused the wreath hanging beside the Police Station door to sway slightly.

Every policeman reporting for the day rainy shift walked past it. The force was reduced by one on Wednesday. And his name was Jim McKnight.

He started out 29 years ago walking a beat and he ended up walking a beat. He was jailer for awhile and squad car patrolman. You can read it on the personal record they took out of the files and marked "deceased."

What you won't find in the files is the way they felt about Jim McKnight—the others on the force: the storekeepers along Central Ave. where he was sent when he grew too tired to pound the midtown pavement; and the kids.

Especially the kids. Helping them across the street on their way to school and home again eventually became Jim McKnight's chief duty. Bad weather or good, he was there. Afterwards, he might stop into the barber shop to rest his feet. But when the kids needed the traffic stopped, Jim McKnight stopped it.

His wasn't a glamorous career. The oldest officers couldn't

remember when he had ever used the pistol that hung at his side. He was quiet and reserved and loyal and even when sick, as he was in his later years.

When some of the youngsters stopped on Central Ave. to ask the new policeman where Mr. McKnight was and he told them, they went away not understanding exactly how it happened or why, but somehow feeling sad.

"Everybody felt that way," one policeman said. "Jim never had much to say but you were always glad to see him come around. He was the first man I met when I came here. He went out of his way to help me. Never said anything, you know, but just did everything he could for me. That's the way he was ... "

That's the way he was. Just for the record, it ought to be said they miss him out on Central Ave. and down at the station.

And that if he could have, Officer James E. McKnight would have been out there stopping traffic for the kids in the damp Wednesday wind that touched his wreath on the station door.

Certain Lady Has Firm Grip On Hand Of Grocer Fincher

October 22, 1956

I F W.B. FINCHER EVER VISITS MONTE CARLO they'd better hide the roulette wheels.

"I'm just plain lucky," he says, and that's like Kim Novak saying, "I'm kinda pretty."

W.B. Fincher is the man who wins things.

It started with a telephone call four or five years ago. It was a lady calling his Central Ave. grocery store. She picked his name at random, because the folks on "Truth or Consequences" told her she had to get an East Coast grocer to deliver her a can of peas. In California.

W.B. Fincher picked up a can of peas and went west. When he got there, they gave him some money and a refrigerator and a silver service and a television set.

Since then, it's been hard to hold W.B. Fincher down.

"I went to the grocers' national convention," he says, a little vaguely. "I put my name in the hat and won another silver service.

"So I got to putting my name in for door prizes and things—nothing that takes any work to do.

"At the state grocers' convention in Greensboro, I won an

air conditioner.

"At last year's national convention, I won a year's supply of spices.

"I've won about four outdoor grills.

"I've won so many magazines and sets of sheets I can't even remember them all.

"I can't lose. I'm afraid people get mad at me sometimes. I just drop my name in, and somebody always pulls it out.

"I didn't enter anything for a while and then last week I went to the county grocers' meeting.

"I figured I'd see how my luck was holding up.

"So I dropped my name in the bucket.

"I won a boat and motor.

"And a trailer to put it on."

Some Day They'll Fill The Shell Of The Church On Cemetery St.

October 23, 1956

O UT AT THE CORNER of Carmel St. and Cemetery St. in Biddleville, there is an empty shell of a church.

They've been building it for 15 years in their hearts. It is finished except for the inside.

This big, empty church is known as Gethsemane AME Zion. One of these days it will have a floor and a roof and a ceiling and be filled with people—and not just ordinary people, but people with loyalty and generosity beyond the normal degree.

They wanted a church, a brick church. They thought about it every time they crowded inside the tiny wooden structure that stood on the spot.

Dr. Walter R. Lovell thought about it, and his family gave a hundred dollars. W.H. Little's small contracting firm tore down the old church and built a larger temporary building. Mrs. Beulah D. Moore and Rev. F.M. Allen led the fight for the money week after week.

The money came in crumpled dollar bills and slowly. The members of Gethsemane AME Zion Church are not wealthy people.

The church conference gave $3,000. The extension

department gave $2,200. The members borrowed as much as they could, individually, from banks and loan companies.

The years passed, May, 1956, came and they decided it was time to build. So they built. The money was just enough to finish the brickwork, the roof and marble steps.

They're still worshipping in a wooden building out at Gethsemane AME Zion Church. They will need $35,000 more to buy their pews and lights and stained glass window and plaster and floorboards.

That is a lot of money, and it may take another 15 years to find it.

But they will find it, and they will walk up the marble steps and into a church of their own someday.

It has taken 15 years to build a shell, but where there are loyalty and dedication and generosity to stretch that far, there will be enough crumpled dollar bills to stretch farther.

Name And Address? Frantic Registrar Just Has To Guess

October 24, 1956

T HEY CLOSED THE REGISTRATION BOOKS YESTERDAY, and just in time.

Mrs. Ruth Fortenbery, the normally cool, genial and efficient registrar, has stood up under some stampedes in her time but this one nearly drove her to the looney cage. People, Mrs. Fortenbery long since discovered are even funnier than politicians. There are numerous chapters and verses to support this text, but two will suffice.

There was the old man a few months ago who wanted to vote, but couldn't tell the folks in the election office just which district he lived in.

In fact, he wasn't sure exactly which street he lived on.

In fact, he didn't know which side of town it was.

Mrs. Fortenbery, with the persistence of Rip Kirby, put the old fellow in her car and had him take her to his house.

"All right," she said, dropping him off there, "you vote at Berryhill School."

Election day rolled around and word came in from the precinct. The old guy had showed up all right, been given a ballot and directed to a voting booth.

Fifteen minutes passed and he hadn't come back to drop his ballot in the box. So they went looking for him.

They found he had lost his way.

He was waiting for someone to help him mark his ballot—in the restroom.

This was as nothing compared to the lady with all the aliases.

She had so many names Mrs. Fortenbery couldn't figure out which one to put on the registration form.

Finally, in desperation, Mrs. Fortenbery took one last stab at it.

"Look," she said, "if you were writing me a letter, how would you sign it?"

The answer came back instantly.

"Love, Lillian," the lady said.

One In The Kisser Worth Two In The Hot Dog Stand

October 25, 1956

Here was this downcast young citizen drowning his sorrow in chocolate milk at Bob Green's hot dog stand on 4th St.

"It's a dirty shame," he said.

"That's right," Bob Green said. "You evermore hit it on the head that time, little buddy," he said.

Bob Green, who is used to customers with problems, is good at sympathizing.

"All I was doing," the young man said, "was taking a drag in the doggone locker room."

He took a cigarette out, regarded it sadly and lit it.

"They let the girls do it," he said. "The girls do it all the time."

"Yeah," Bob Green said. "I know they do."

"Nobody ever says nothin' about that," the young man said.

He took a long, thoughtful puff of the cigarette.

"I figured I had time for a quick smoke between classes," he said. "That doggone principal had been saying he was going to do something rash, but nobody believed him."

"Didn't think he meant it, huh?" Bob Green said.

"Nope," the young man said. "So me and this other boy were standing at the door getting one last drag, and when the door opened, naturally we had to exhale."

"That's when it hit him, huh?" Bob Green asked.

"Right in the face," the young man said. He shuddered to think about it.

"And he kicked you out, huh?" Bob Green asked.

"For a week," the young man said. "For a solid week. The other guy figured he didn't see his face, so he went and changed his shirt."

"But they got him, too," Bob Green said.

"Both of us," the young man said.

"Have another chocolate milk," Bob Green said.

Face Lifter Deluxe Returns For Shot At Another Counter

October 26, 1956

W. H. McWhirter, more than any other man we can think of, has changed the face of the city.

He started 34 years ago, and for most of the time since he has been off face-lifting such other corners of the globe as Quito, Ecuador; Panama City, Panama; Norfolk, Va., and wherever else the far-flung interests of the J.A. Jones Construction Co. dictated.

But he is a Charlotte man and there is hardly a street in this town W. H. McWhirter can stroll along without passing some monument to his career.

He is superintending the construction of the 15-story Wachovia building at Trade and Church Sts. right now. Mr. Mac took time the other day to list the other Charlotte buildings he has erected for J.A. Jones.

Taking them one at a time:

"The Hotel Charlotte.

"The City Hall group, both of those with Raymond Jones.

"The Wilder building.

"The Addison apartments.

"The Addison building.

"The Duke Power building.

"The Queen College dormitories and gym.

"And—a number of church and school buildings.

"All that was 23 years ago or longer. I left Charlotte for other jobs in 1933 ... "

He looked over the skeleton frame of the skyscraper-to-be before him, almost ready to rise above the street.

"I'm right glad they brought me back for this one," he said.

"Manufacturing buildings are the most satisfying to put up, because you have all this machinery to play with. This building is hard—you have no place to store materials. It's given us a good deal of trouble, but it will be a beautiful building.

"I was married at the time we built the Hotel Charlotte. We were five stories up with concrete, as I recall.

"The Wilder was my first one alone. I remember we had to put a penthouse on the top because Mrs. Wiley, whose house had been on the spot, insisted on it. The penthouse is still there, but no one is living in it now ... "

He paused to flick the ashes from his cigar.

"Yes, I've been working in Georgia, Alabama, Florida, South Carolina, Washington state ... I built the big hospital at Chapel Hill and the Liggett and Myers building in Durham ...

"But it's good to be back in Charlotte."

And good, one surmised, to be altering Charlotte in a steel and concrete way that will outlive the youngest child who now stands on tiptoes to stare at the construction through the barricade at Trade and Church Sts.

Return Of The Pitchman Stops Bug-Eyed Dime Store Onlookers

October 29, 1956

F OR A WHILE THERE, we thought the pitchman had passed into history with medicine shows, but friends, we couldn't have been more wrong.

For there she was, friends, with flaming red hair, a throaty come-on, two spotlights, a microphone and a rapid-fire patter line that had the crowd around the store counter eating out of her hand.

"Step right up, friends," she said. "I have a little hair preparation here I'd like to demonstrate. If you can't step right up, lie down and get outta the way ... "

She grinned, they grinned, it was wonderful.

"Now the American people are the most intelligent people in the world," she said. "And if you don't believe it, ask the one next to you ... "

A little old wide-eyed lady with a shopping bag edged closer, hanging on every word.

"I was driving down from New York," the redhead said, "and I saw a sign—Burials $99.98—but you know what it said in the little teeny print? 'This month only.' You die this month, you get a bargain, next month, it'll cost you one hundred bucks ... "

She handed out free samples, one at a time, building the crowd.

"Alcohol won't grow hair, friends," she said. "If your barber says it will, take a good long look at his own head—probably bald ...

"Nothing, nothing, nothing in this world will grow hair where there is none," she said. "If alcohol would grow hair, there'd be a lot of guys with fur-lined stomachs. I know 'em and you do too ... "

The little old lady nodded agreement and smiled. The redhead burned a little alcohol, rubbed her hands in goosegrease.

She named a movie queen. "You've admired those long, flowing tresses?"

She raised her eyebrows.

"Bald as a billiard ball," she said, and the little old lady gasped.

"Now you've all heard a lot about Lanolin," the redhead said. "On the radio, the TV, the newspapers, you're probably sick to death of Lanolin ...

"Well, now, let me tell you about this little package I have before me. To pure, governmental Lanolin, we've added oil of eucalyptus, oxiquinaline sulphate and sulphur, and we've been at one address, 1119 Boardwalk, Atlantic City, N.J., friends, for 19 long years ... "

The little old lady turned to the person next to her and said, earnestly:

"She'd make a good preacher."

We never found out what she was selling, but friends, it was magnificent.

Portrait For The Fall

October 30, 1956

W ALKING THE STREETS:

The clarity and cleanliness of fall extends even to the city, or is it just imagination that gives the suggestion of a smile to the faces of the people you meet, and zing to their step?

A happy, tattered citizen loads fall leaves on a truck on Trade St. and sings a gospel song as he works:

"Oh, Lord, pity me, a sinner ... "

But the man doesn't look like a sinner. He is at peace with the world and the evidence is on his overall jacket—one Jones button, one Stevenson button, and a United Appeal emblem, symbol of his contribution to the unfortunates of Mecklenburg: Those who can't load leaves and sing.

Fall means different things to different people.

For Bill Hodges, Charlotte's young man with a horn, it is a season of success. Next week, he'll load himself and his trumpet on an airplane in New York. He will help the Benny Goodman band flip the jazz bugs at one-nighters in Bangkok, Hong Kong and Jakarta.

For the blind youngster mentioned in this space two weeks ago, the one who wanted a record player, it is a season of happiness. A number of people found they had record players they could spare, and one of them, a brand new one, is in his room right now.

For one woman, at least, it is a season of sadness. She stood on the corner of 4th and Church under yesterday's murky skies and cried. Another woman stopped and asked her, "Is there anything I can do for you?" She shook her head, buried her face in a handkerchief and hurried away—why, or to where, we do not know.

The important thing, of course, is that somebody stopped and tried to help.

The important thing is that somebody gave a record player to a blind boy who wanted one, that Bill Hodges is going to blow for the Bangkok jazz fans, that the trash collector could sing.

On the carefully manicured lawn of the First Presbyterian Church, there is one bare spot. Suspended over it is an old tire for children to swing on.

You pass it on a fall day, and this, too, becomes an important thing—one further proof that the City of Churches hasn't forgotten its Christianity.

World's Greatest Shine Boy

October 31, 1956

I WOULD NOT SAY," Scoop said, "that I am the world's greatest shoeshine boy.

"But I have heard it said."

If not the world's greatest shoeshine boy, Wilford (Scoop) Antley is among the greatest talkers. Scoop can talk. He can hardly get the shoes shined town at Tate Barber Shop on 4th St. for talking.

"I am a professional," Scoop said. "I am now 35 years old, and I started when I was 10. I'm better now than I've ever been. I'm at my peak, you might say."

He popped the rag, like the professional he is.

"I started out toting a shine box at the Selwyn Hotel. Those were the days when the law used to run us up the street if we didn't have a license. I believe I had a license."

He squirted shoe cream out of an oil can.

"That's the secret," he said. "Plenty of shoe cream, plenty of elbow grease. I take shoes like they come. Lots of boys don't like two tones. Shining two tones comes to me like chewing this tobacco."

Scoop popped the rag again.

"Some people want their shoes shined. Some just want the rag popped. I do both. I never get tired bending over. I'm just as limber as this rag."

He brushed on the sole dressing.

"The only pair of shoes I ever messed up on," he said, "was a pair of light tan shoes when I was nothing but a boy. Got dark spots on 'em, and I never forgot it. Since then ... "

Scoop straightened up and looked demurely at the sfloor ...

"Since then," he said, "I've been pretty hard to stop."

November 1956

———

He told us a great deal about ourselves, because he essentially was Everyman.

—Julian Scheer,
reporter, *Charlotte News*

Crowd Gathered In The Dark

November 1, 1956

T HE CROWD GATHERED IMMEDIATELY.

It formed a tight ring around the girl lying on the Tryon St. sidewalk, jostled for a good position to look at her, stood aimlessly, waiting for something to happen, listening for the siren it knew was coming.

And the people in the crowd, like people in every crowd in every town in every circumstance, talked.

"She jumped?" a wide-eyed man asked. "Did she jump?"

A man from the grocery store nearby looked at him scornfully.

"No," he said.

A worried lady pushed her way to the inside of the crowd and peered down at the face of the girl, with the color just coming back to her cheek.

"Ohhh," she said, loud enough for everybody to hear. "I thought it was Mrs. Williams."

A lady came out of the ring of people, knelt down and tenderly took the girl's head in her lap. A man spread an overcoat over her.

A minute before, all these people had been hurrying

down the street. Now, they were in no hurry. The interruption of normality, the fact that other people had stopped, that something had happened, stopped them also.

Their faces turned toward the face of the girl, showing real concern, or showing intense, unashamed, obvious, vulgar curiosity about what misfortune had overtaken her, what condition had brought her to the sidewalk this way.

A teen-aged boy left his girl friend standing on the edge of the growing crowd, edged into it, came back and spoke confidently, clearing up the mystery.

"I think she was hit by a car."

"Oh," his girl friend said.

The siren finally came. It was a police car. The young cop on the corner stopped the traffic and an older, experienced officer opened the car door, strode through the crowd and knelt at the girl's side.

"I was right here, when she fell down," a fat man was telling two or three other people. "I called the ambulance," he said.

"She was a pretty thing, wasn't she?" a lady said.

"I think she just fainted, Billy," the teenaged girl was telling her boyfriend.

"Maybe so," he said.

The crowd was gone. Normality rushed in to take its place on the corner. The salesman went back inside the car, the police car pulled away from the curb.

A lady who had run into a friend in the crowd asked her, "Do you think you and Ed could come to supper Friday night?"

The Dying Breed

November 2, 1956

S HED A TEAR FOR THE CHAUFFEUR.

Like the Twelve Wired King Bird Of New Guinea, the chauffeur is a dying breed.

We cannot decide who to blame for this phenomenon— Roosevelt, perhaps. But no matter. The chauffeur is on his way out.

Consider the plight. After delivering his mistress to her destination (as the solitary chauffeur on Tryon St. the other afternoon had done) he must stand and wait.

He cannot even commiserate with others of his calling. There are none.

There was a time when it was not so. There was a time when the spotless, liveried masters of the motorcar could congregate on the spa at Newport; could perhaps even quaff a brew in the jolly fellowship while their assorted employers waxed genteel under the chandeliers.

It is gone, all gone.

The lonely chauffeur on Tryon St. had nobody to talk to, except one acquaintance who happened by for a minute.

"Do you get much hunting done?" the acquaintance

asked him.

"Haven't had no time," the chauffeur said.

Of course, it was true. The man is doubtless gardener, butler and handyman as well as chauffeur. The Packard is his domain, yes, but not exclusively. Nothing is exclusive any more.

That is what America has come to, and there is nothing that can be done about it.

A little girl, brought up ignorant in the new democracy, passed our chauffeur on Tryon St., holding the hand of the other phone.

"Daddy," she asked, "why is that man dressed like that?"

When you are the last of your kind, you must be prepared for such things.

Questions, But No Answers

November 5, 1956

S MALL QUESTIONS:

"I ain't kiddin' you, Paul. She's the prettiest girl in town, and about once a week, she goes sleep-walking. They picked her up last night—in PURPLE pajamas."

Who?

Mrs. Ethel Sloop, one of the most selfless ladies in this selfish world, needs help again.

She's been running her "Over 40" club, the non-profit employment club for older workers from a church office. Now, the church needs the room for basketball—and Mrs. Sloop needs an office.

Her club was founded when Mrs. Sloop, a book-keeper, found she couldn't get a job because of her age. She's been fighting a good fight every since, has placed some 300 workers—all "over 40"—in productive jobs.

The "Over 40" Club has no dues. So Mrs. Sloop can pay no rent.

But she must have an office.

Where?

One of the first things Miss Helen McManus used

to teach her ignorant English students down at Central High School was not to say "let" when you mean "leave."

But Miss Mac, the hornet's nest bolted to the monument in front of the Courthouse bears this deathless warning:

"Let us alone!"

Why?

Magazine editors are buggier than newspaper people, even, and will bend further out of joint for a story, to wit:

Title of the lead piece in the current *Chemical Week* is, "The Chemical Angle To Next Week's Election."

What?

The dolls in Belk's window attracted two little girls, poorly dressed little girls with thin faces and stringy hair.

They contrasted pitifully with the plump, polished, clean and frilly girls of plastic and lace in the window.

One of the youngsters pointed to the largest, prettiest doll and said, "My Daddy is going to get me that one."

Her friend look at her, not believing it. Then, in the straightforward and cruel manner of children, she asked the one question the little girl couldn't answer:

"When?"

The Great Debate

November 6, 1956

A SERIOUS QUESTION HAS ARISEN in the neighborhood of Joe Zappalorto's Service Newsstand.

Is Wilford (Scoop) Antley after all, the city's shoeshine king?

Joe's candidate: Leroy (Horsefly) Simpson.

We advanced Scoop in this space last week as a strong contender for the honor after he claimed he  had heard it said he was the greatest, not only in this area, but in the world.

This is too wide a territory, according to the bent, gold-toothed Mr. Simpson, who says he has been at his calling for 35 years, 10 years longer than the younger Mr. Antley.

"As a matter of fact," he said ominously, "he comes down here wanting to learn my tricks."

This clearly calls for some reconsideration.

"Look here," Mr. Simpson said, pressing his point. "Everybody in town can tell you about ol' Horsefly. People come from 12 miles around just to have me shine their shoes. Man, I'm common knowledge.

"I worked for 20 years for the Greek up on the Square. Before that, I carried a shoeshine box. There ain't nobody can tell me nothing about shining shoes.

"I have more regular customers than anybody else. I have bigger tips than most. It took me 10 years to get good—I mean real good—and now sometimes the customers have to stand in line."

Mr. Simpson paused in this "recitative" for Mr. Zappalorto to say, "He's terrific."

"And I ain't scared of nobody," Mr. Simpson said.

Accordingly, there is to be a shoeshining contest in the next few days, pitting Mr. Antley ("Scoop" to his friends) and Mr. Simpson ("Horsefly" to his) in mortal combat with brushes and cloths. It is to be a competition of some magnitude and will settle this matter once and for all.

Judges will be Waldo (The Glim) Proffitt, city editor of the *News*, who got his eagle eye through years of practice on typographical errors; and "Big John" Hildreth of our composing room, whose shoes, frankly, need the shine.

Time and place to be announced.

The Faces Of Freedom

November 7, 1956

W HO CAN FORGET THE FACE OF A FREE MAN?

From Hungary, we have seen such faces of late. The wirephoto process has transmitted their hope and their agony across the miles—from the men dying for freedom in the streets of Budapest to the neat neighborhoods of America, from which other men have  gone forth to die for freedom, and will again.

The wrinkled face of a machine-gunned Hungarian patriot is not unlike the wrinkled face of a Huntersville farmer preparing to drop a ballot in a ballot box on an American election day.

There is a kinship. And who can forget such a face?

Quiet came yesterday to both Hungary and Huntersville. For the patriot, it meant his desperate, hopeless revolution has been crushed. For the farmer, it meant that the tumult and the shouting of an American election was over; that is was time to vote.

Two such different meanings were born, however, of the same idea. It is not an easy idea to express. Perhaps neither the patriot nor the farmer could express it.

But they feel it, they know it, both of them.

It has to do with such names as Jefferson and Mindszenty, Yankee and Magyar, Lexington and Budapest, with such tools as rifles and newspapers and pulpits and ballot boxes.

Both of them understand that.

Both of them—the Huntersville farmer who voted with his aged mother yesterday, and the Hungarian street fighter who lost his last battle yesterday—were thinking about it.

This is the thing that transcends the result of the American election and the failure of the Hungarian revolution.

This is the thing you could have read in their faces.

And once having seen such a face, who can forget it?

'It Was Never Easy'

November 8, 1956

D AY IS GONE,
Gone the sun,
From the earth,
From the hills,
From the sky . . .

"It was never easy," Carl B. Harris remembers.

"We did it more than 100 times, and it always seemed to take an iron nerve to keep from breaking up."

Carl B. Harris was the bugler who played "Taps" at the military funerals of Mecklenburg servicemen who died in World War II and in the Korean fighting.

With an honor guard and a firing squad from Hornet's Nest Post 9 of the American Legion, Carl B. Harris stood beside 100 graves on 100 of those bitter days and sounded the crisp, sad notes 100 times.

"The first one was at Mint Hill cemetery," he recalls. "That may have been the first military funeral in Mecklenburg County. First the honor guard, then the volley, then 'Taps.'

"It was never any fun. It was never easy, either. We were

glad to do it, of course, but ...

"It was the last notes that were the hardest. I hope I don't have to play them again."

So to sleep,
Safely rest,
God is nigh.

Starlight In The Alley

November 9, 1956

OF ALL THE JOBS IN THIS
TOWN, the most thankless
belongs to those who comb
the alleys for bottles and
boxes. They pull rickety
wooden carts through the
streets to gain a dollar or
two a day, a small reward
in a prosperous era.

For most of these men,
pasteboard box collecting is
a vocation, a means of live-

lihood. Like most enterprises, it is competitive. Those who
search for boxes in the little-traveled corners of the city know
what time Sterchi's discards its pasteboard the way secretaries
know what time the boss gives dictation.

Eleven-year-old Charles Simpson and his brother Lira, 8,
are not professionals, however. They are new at the game.
They started just two months ago.

"We generally do it after school," Charles explained. "We

get 60 cents per hundred pounds for the boxes down at the mill. We get five cents for drink jugs when they have tops on 'em and three cents when they don't. We sell them to the juice place."

Charles and his brother built their own cart with cast-off lumber and Soap Box Derby wheels.

"Some days," he says, "we don't hardly make nothing. Some days we make maybe a dollar. We take it home to Mama.

"We save some of it, too. I want to grow up and cut hair and Lira don't know what he wants to do yet, but something like that. Mama says I got my eye on a star, but I'll do it."

The two boys have worked hard at the job, but they have the problems amateurs are bound to have.

"We don't know when the cartons are thrown out," Charles says. "That's the biggest trouble. If we knew, we'd be there, but we haven't learned about it yet. We just have to be lucky and do the best we can."

Charles and Lira Simpson's best will someday be good enough, likely. Every man who starts out collecting boxes for 60 cents a hundred pounds doesn't end up cutting hair, it is true.

But then every man who walks in the alleys doesn't have his eye on a star.

Of Basic Thought

November 12, 1956

AT 1110 DILWORTH RD. E. on Mondays and Thursdays, a class is conducted.

The people in the classroom can speak and write perfectly well, but they speak and write Greek, Chinese, Polish, Japanese, Spanish and French. At 1110 Dilworth Rd. E., they are learning English.

Their teachers are volunteers, their tuition is free. The school is run by B'nai B'rith for immigrants who want to become citizens.

The teachers don't know the language of their students in most cases.

"This," they say, "is a light." Or "This is a desk." They write it on the blackboard. They repeat it. Their students copy it laboriously and try to say it: "This is a light."

All these students have is a pencil, paper and determination. They have a lot to learn. They do not know about the vast rolling hills of America or its forests or farms. Most of them do not know about so elementary an American thing as the motion picture, in most cases. Their America is the street on which they work and the street on which they live.

One of their teachers is Dora Washam.

"In America," she tells them pointing to a map, "we have liberty."

Liberty is a word they know.

"We have liberty of speech," pointing to her mouth, "liberty of press," pointing to a newspaper, "liberty of religion," folding her hands in the attitude of one in prayer.

This they understand. We have had freedom of speech for 180 years. The Greeks had it 3,000 years ago.

"In America," Mrs. Washam says, "one man," pointing to one of her students, "is as good as another man."

So it goes. And a young Chinese housewife, a Greek airplane mechanic, a French textile engraver strains to comprehend.

"This is elementary and slow, very slow," Mrs. Washam says. "But it's not a job for an agency with a lot of money. It's a job for people who know you have to extend the torch of freedom to others to keep it burning."

The torch of freedom is passed down these multilingual aisles.

"Nick has his business," Mrs. Washam says, writing it out. "John will have his business." She is trying to teach the elements of present and future tense. But John does not understand it that way.

"Yes," he says, haltingly. "John will have."

Street Corners

November 13, 1956

S TREET CORNERS:

A thin young woman in a threadbare coat stood on the corner of S. Tryon and W. 4th Sts. in last Saturday's cold wind.

She was there, leaning against the granite wall of the bank at 7 a.m., waiting. At 11 o'clock, when the high-stepping majorettes in the scanty suits and the flag-bearing Legionnaires marched up Tryon St. in the Veterans Day parade, she hardly gave them a glance.

At three in the afternoon, she was still there, sitting on the ledge on the 4th St. side to shield herself from the wind. Her dark eyes followed every car, every person who passed the corner.

When the midtown workers had all gone home and the early moviegoers were on their way down Tryon St., she was gone, and the paperboy on the corner answered the question:

"She said she was waiting for somebody.

"But she left by herself."

The best named street corner in town is Church and

Trade, where the smoke-clad steeple of First Presbyterian Church has a growing rival—the Wachovia Bank Building, now at street height but soon to rise high above the steeple, a 15-story citadel of Trade.

Most gregarious corner is 4th and Mint, where laborers congregate every morning at dawn to stamp their feet on the chilly pavement and wait for would-be employers to pass and pick them up. They dicker for a moment on the day's wages, strike a deal and climb aboard, subjects of the city's most informal collective bargaining.

Happiest corner is N. Tryon and 5th—where Santa Claus has made his first appearance in the Ivey's window.

Loneliest corner is a block away at Tryon and 6th. Vacant plate glass windows bear the pasty remnants of a bold sign that said, "All The Way With Adlai." The headlines a week ago told the story. The busy office is empty now. Nobody has been inside for seven days—except to take down the signs and put up a new one.

"For Rent."

A Railroading Man

November 14, 1956

NOT LONG AGO IN THIS SPACE we were shedding tears over the Younger Generation's preoccupation with space ships to the exclusion of sensible things like trains.

Happily, there is an exception to ever rule. The exception to this one is Casey Clifford.

When Casey (whose proper handle is "Bob") wants to get home to 327 Atherton St. from town on Saturday afternoons, he just moseys down to the Southern station, finds a switch engine going his way, and rides. They let him off a block from his house.

Casey—so named by classmates at Central High—knows every engineer, every conductor and every rail liner who makes the ancient depot his headquarters.

His basement room at home has six electric trains, yards of track and more trusses and signal flags than you'd likely find in a well equipped storage house beside the mainline tracks.

Down at Johney's Hobby House, the model railroad's local Mecca, they've gotten so they consult Casey whenever they're in doubt about a price or a stock number.

Casey Clifford just can't stay away from trains. While his friends are whooping it up for the Wildcats on the football field, old Casey is likely to be up at the roundhouse in Spencer, poking around and asking questions.

While his friends are reading funny books and fan magazines, Casey's at home, absorbed in "Ties," the Southern's official publication.

Spaceships are for the birdmen. Casey Clifford is lost in the artifacts and drama and folklore of the railroad.

The other day, he brought a doorstep home to his family. A 50-pound iron spring from a steam engine.

Portrait Of An Artist

November 15, 1956

W HEN YOU WALK UP THE STAIRS to the second floor of Charlotte's new library at the Saturday open house, you will come face to face with five paintings.

They are the crisp, imaginative expressions of Murray Whisnant. Offhand, we would guess the town may someday be proud to be called his home.

At 24, Murray Whisnant, a quiet, loose-jointed redhead who doodled his way through Central High School and drew national attention to the State College School of Design, is already close to the front rank of young American painters.

Unlike talented businessmen of his age, talented artists draw attention only in tight circles. Also, they don't make much money.

So Murray Whisnant is a designer for the Charlotte architects' firm of Sloan & Wheatley. By day, he designs additions to fire escapes. By night, he paints.

"It's a way of staying in shape," he says. "In architecture, there is constant discipline and compromise. You can't always do what you want because, you know, somebody else is paying for it. In painting, of course, you're free."

That is the longest paragraph anybody is likely to get out of Murray Whisnant. He does his talking with a brush.

Why did he choose the "modern" approach to his work instead of conforming to the "pretty" tradition of white rail fences, cows in meadows, sailships at docks at sunset?

"I ... just wanted to."

Because he just wanted to, Murray Whisnant is building a ladder for himself over the high wall that separates real painters from the Christmas card variety.

A committee of judges recommended purchase of one of his paintings for the new state art museum.

His State College tutors speak of him with uncommon respect.

Old Conrad Aiken, the poet who knows what he likes, liked one of Murray Whisnant's paintings well enough to take it home and hang it on the wall.

And this weekend's one man show in the library is his latest success.

For the Murray Whisnants of this world, though, "success" is a funny word. It comes in funny ways and it doesn't have much to do with newspaper stories or dollar marks.

It has to do, again, with saying things, with a brush or a pen or a horn or a chisel.

Go down and look at Murray Whisnant's paintings this weekend. Maybe you'll find them talking to you.

No. 4 Head Please, Bwana

November 16, 1956

Y OU HAVE NOTED THOSE LINES OF TYPE in an otherwise intelligible newspaper story that say, "etaoin shrdlu?"

Just Art Yates lapsing into Mau Mau.

At such times, needless to say, he is of little use to *The Charlotte News* copy desk. With all the trouble in that part of the world, our Mau Mau subscriptions have dwindled to practically nothing.

But it is hard to express just how much it means to have a Mau Mau man around the office, especially one who has a nodding acquaintance with Zulu, Bechuana, Matebeles and Liuwhuwie dialects as well.

The demand of geology and the U.S. Army combined to take Art Yates into cobwebby corners of the world which you and I, alas, may never see.

But we can sit at the knee of this 26-year-old Marco Polo, we can lean starry eyed on the rim of the desk, and listen to him name the exotic parts of his memory:

Sudbury, Caracas, London, Poughkeepsie. That brings him up to the age of 17. Then Johannesburg, Capetown, Tunis, Kano, Leopoldville, Accra, Dakar (break out the rum and dagger, Bwana, we're headed for the interior), Mozambique, Kenya, Uganda, Tanganyika. Then Karlsruhe, Germany. Then Asia. Then Hollywood, California. Then Spearfish, South Dakota.

We are not kidding you, gentle reader. You can see this boy has been in training all his life to become a *Charlotte News* copyreader.

Along the way, he dived for pearls off Margarita Island, cracked up in a C-47 in Cumaho, Venezuela, got chased by a rhinoceros in Krugar National Park and flew through the mists of Victoria Falls.

But enough. The old heart is pounding too fast to go on. If you have ever hauled out a road map and contemplated with concern the distance from Charlotte to Gastonia, you know the feeling.

Still, we can but admire Art Yates, we who only dream of the Transvaal and the Nile.

And if he can just work that *shrdlue* thing into English, there'll be no stopping him in the newspaper game.

Voice of Democracy

November 19, 1956

THIRTEEN HIGH SCHOOL BOYS AND GIRLS stood up in a WIST studio the other night to say what democracy means to them.

They said it well.

See the American people as they hurry to the churches of their choice, said Lena Helton of J.H. Gunn School. *Look now, as they go about their daily occupations ...*

This was the annual "Voice of Democracy" contest, sponsored by the Jaycees, in which a million American youngsters each year sit down and think and write and speak for democracy.

My fathers were witch doctors and primitive savages, slaves and masters of slaves, were kings and peons, nobles and untouchables.

Carolyn Settle Chase of Central High School speaking.

My fathers were Socrates, Joan of Arc, Benjamin Franklin,

Thomas Jefferson, Abraham Lincoln ...

We have still to light the blindness of prejudice, to wipe out the blight of ignorance, to blow away the cobwebs of untruth which devour men's minds ...

Clearly democracy is more than a word in an encyclopedia to Lena Helton and Carolyn Chase. To Sue Hill of Myers Park High School too:

And the dream took hold of men ... and would not die. Democracy is a boy climbing a flagpole and the flag spreading her shadow upon him and waving there high above him.

Democracy is driving home late at night through a fine rain, past the corner of the Methodist Church ...

Democracy is a hot, sleepy Sabbath in a small Southern town ... Democracy is the dim upper stacks of the library at night ...

Democracy is sitting on the school terrace with the exchange student from Germany and watching the fiery red fade to mauve behind the black trees and wanting badly to know whether sunsets are the same everywhere.

No political orator or any flag-draped politician is likely to come any closer than that.

The Contest Takes Shape

November 20, 1956

IT'S A FUNNY TOWN:

The Great Shoeshining Contest will be held at Joe Zappalorto's Service Newsstand, 402 S. Tryon St., at 3:30 tomorrow afternoon.

It will pit Scoop Antley of Tate's Barbershop against Horsefly Simpson, the aging challenger who works at the newsstand. One fall to a finish.

With Scoop claiming to be the world's greatest shoeshine boy and Horsefly the only dissenter, the scope of the contest becomes clear. The wire services and national magazines have been duly notified.

We wish to announce the addition of Sandy "Chatanoogi Shoe Shine" Grady to the list of judges. Mr. Grady is a veteran of Soap Box Derbys and Volkswagen road races and a man of unimpeachable eyesight when he has his glasses on. He joins Waldo "The Glim" Proffitt and "Big John" Hildreth on the shoeshine stand.

The contestants are ready.

"I'm nervous as a honey bee," Mr. Antley confided just yesterday. "I want to get it over."

"I'll take him," said Mr. Simpson, a man of few words.

This is to be a contest in the modern manner of judging on the following basis: Glitter—85 points; Technique—10 points; Rag Popping and Incidental Conversation—5 points.

Decision of the judges is final.

We have a postscript story on Bob Clifford, the Central High sophomore who is buggy about trains.

The day after his story appeared here, Bob and his family were out riding in their car.

They came to a Southern railroad crossing. The engineer of a slow moving train on the tracks recognized Bob, a crippled youngster who spends most of his spare time down at the station.

So instead of stopping for the train—the train stopped for them.

A beauteous blonde babe in a red dress hopped into a W. Trade St. cafe the other night, causing eight or ten patrons to nearly choke on their beer. She smiled her way down the aisle to expressions of admiration coming from either side, walked up to an old citizen sitting at a back stool, kissed him on his bald dome without a word and tripped out.

There was a stunned silence.

The old guy grinned like crazy, and refused to tell anybody anything.

'One Little Thing I Can Do'

November 21, 1956

F RED PARKER, a North Belmont citizen who has spent all his life working in a textile mill, has discovered he can cheer people up.

This was a discovery of some importance to a man who previously was concerned only with caring for his sick wife and working his way up from the weaving room.

His talent is unique.

He explains, "I practiced it up myself."

Fred Parker can touch his chin with his nose.

He knows nobody else in the world who can touch his chin with his nose. He found he could do it while waiting for false teeth to come in.

"I was just fooling around," he says, "and I got my chin and nose touching there, and my boy got to laughing. Then I went up to the mill and the boys laughed too. So now I do it around town and around the mill villages."

Fred Parker cannot sing, he cannot dance, he does not tell jokes. He just clamps a hat on his head, pulls his glasses down low and touches his chin with his nose.

People laugh.

"There was this 17-year-old girl over at the Presbyterian Hospital," Fred Parker says, "and she wanted to die. So I started going over there. I'd borrow a hat from somebody and do it for her. I really do believe she's getting on better now.

"And then there were these relatives down in Greer, South Carolina, and an old gentleman up home. I cheer everybody up that I can. It's just one little thing I can do."

Fred Parker's biggest promoter is his son, Franklin Delano Parker. Franklin Delano laughs fit to kill every time his daddy touches his chin with his nose.

"And," Fred Parker adds, "I have touched my chin with my nose for the Wilkinson Boulevard Volunteer Fire Department, the Free Will Baptist Church and the Patriotic Order Sons of America. I belong to all them.

"But I will do it for anybody. I just want to cheer people up. If anybody needs my services at any time, I will be only too glad to oblige."

'Only One Thing To Do'

November 22, 1956

OUT OF THE MISTS OF YESTERDAY'S MORNING, a man stumbled.

"Do you have a cigarette?" he asked.

He took it matter-of-factly, as if he had it coming to him, as if this were a little enough thing, after all.

"I been up all night," he said. "Sure, I been drinking and walking around and trying to figure out what to do."

The only sign of the fact that he was drunk was in his way of looking at the passerby and in his slow, careful way of picking his words.

"There's only one thing to do," he said, "and that's put a bullet in my head, but I don't even have a gun. I could do it, don't think I couldn't do it, man. The only thing I been afraid of is John Law would get me before I could find a gun and do it."

He talked as if the guy who had stopped to give him a cigarette was an old and sympathetic friend, perhaps one who could tell him, "Don't do it, don't be crazy."

"My girl friend got to thinking she was somebody," the man said. "Got to thinking she was too good for me. First I thought I'd shoot her but that wouldn't do no good, would it? I have thought it out, man, first one way and then another and the only way to fix everything up is—"

He stopped short of saying the words again.

"That's the only way out," he said. "Thanks for the cigarette, man. You'll be reading about me in the paper."

He walked off, turned into an alley and disappeared into the fog.

He was just as safe as if he were home in bed.

Any cop will tell you—the ones who are really going to do it don't talk about it first.

The Crazy Shoes Of Taegu

November 23, 1956

AMONG THE ZANIER ATTRACTIONS at the Carrousel ball were the jesters. After the fashion of plain old American clowns, they wore outsized shoes long enough for two or three men.

Those shoes took chief jester Jack Pentes back to other celebrations and another Thanksgiving. It was Korea. 1954. The fighting was over, the cold, wet season had set in and Jack Pentes was an American soldier-artist with a little time on his hands.

He decided the thing to do was to make a clown getup and give the kids in the Taegu orphans' home a Thanksgiving show.

"I went to an old papa-san shoemaker named Hong," Jack Pentes remembers. "He was about 90 years old and he ran his shop in a place the size of an average bathroom, heated with scraps of leather.

"I drew him a picture of the shoes I wanted. He started telling me I was crazy in Korean.

"I'd point to the picture and he'd hold the yardstick down to my shoes and say, 'Crazy, crazy.'

"I just couldn't make him understand why I wanted these

shoes. He'd never heard of a clown before.

"It took me 10 days to get the idea across. I drew a picture of a clown and that even shook him up more. But finally we made a deal. He charged me nine cartons of cigarettes and went to work.

"The word got around the neighborhood, naturally, and the people would come in to watch him working on these shoes on his old rickety sewing machine. They'd shake their heads and mumble, but the old guy made a bargain, and he just let his business slide and worked on these crazy shoes.

"When he finally finished, he put 'em in the window. All the Korean boys came by to look. When I came to pick 'em up, kids followed me. That was the day before Thanksgiving.

"On Thanksgiving Day, I went to the orphans' home. I took Santa Claus with me—it was a little early, but they didn't know the difference. And after the show, I dropped back by the old guy's shop, wearing the clown suit and shoes.

"Then and only then did he know what the shoes were for. Every kid within a two-mile radius was there. Dogs were barking, people were hollering and running out of their houses. It just killed 'em.

"I don't know how many shows we gave. Shoeshine boys were afraid to touch 'em but all the kids had to do was take one look at those shoes and they'd bust out laughing."

Jack Pentes—who now runs Commercial Art Shop on W. 4th St.—was a big hit at the Carrousel ball in old man Hong's long shoes.

But he couldn't help letting his mind wander back to that other Thanksgiving.

They loved him in Taegu.

A Curb's Eye View

November 26, 1956

A THREE-YEAR-OLD'S PARADE:

People—Something that will skwush you if you don't watch out.

Newspapers—Things that keep blowing in your face.

Princesses—Girls way up there high.

Floats—Big shiny things that go swish and sparkle and sometimes a hand waves.

Popcorn—Stuff people drop and you can pick it up and it's good.

Bands—Noise and they try to step on your fingers.

Policemen—They stand still and you can untie their shoelaces and they don't say much.

Horses—Scary animals and they smell bad and they smoke through the nose when it's cold.

Boy Scouts—Big boys that think they're something. And say "Move back."

Hopalong Cassidy—He can beat up anybody except Daddy and Santa Claus.

Sun—What hurts your eyes except somebody always gets back in front of you again and it doesn't hurt your eyes any more but it stops being warm and you can't see nothing.

Clowns—Something that squirts water on Mommy and she says a bad word.

Santa Claus—Everybody talks about him and he'll bring you presents down the chimney and when he comes by everybody hollers but he's looking the other way and you can't think what to holler anyway and the people laugh and go away and the lights are on and you don't want to go home.

Dialogue For A Cold Day

November 27, 1956

THE FIVE-YEAR-OLD STOOD IN SILENCE, his hands in his pockets to keep them warm, while the amateur gardener next door worked the hard ground with a trowel.

"It's cold isn't it?" the five-year-old asked.

The amateur gardener straightened his back for a minute and agreed it was cold.

"I think it's too cold to plant stuff," the five-year-old said.

"Not for bulbs," he said. "They like it cold. You put 'em way down in the ground to keep 'em a little bit warm and they do all right."

"What do they do?" the five-year-old asked.

"They grow," the gardener said, bending to the job again, breaking the hard ground with the trowel.

"What do you get?" he asked. "Do you get tomatoes or flowers?"

"Flowers," the gardener said. "Small flowers called cro-cuses." He showed the boy the picture on the package, red, white and purple flowers.

The five-year-old took a bulb from the package and examined it.

"I sure don't know how it works," he said. "Do you?"

The gardener said, well, no, he didn't exactly know how it worked either.

"Can I help?" the five-year-old asked.

He waited until the amateur gardener had a hole three inches deep. Then slowly, reverently, he put a bulb at the bottom of the hole, scooped loose dirt over it carefully, watching until the bulb and its tiny sprout disappeared, packed the dirt as he had see the gardener do, covered the spot with leaves and pine needles.

"It's not too cold for that one," he said. "Nope. That one will grow. Every day, I'll come see if it's up. Then after it comes up it will get a flower, but we don't know how it works, do we? But the flower will be mine, won't it?

"I'll give it to my mama," he said.

The cold day was suddenly warm.

The International Set

November 28, 1956

T HE INTERNATIONAL SET:

A former member of the Israeli army who now lives in Charlotte stood in front of the new library on Tryon St. the other morning and pondered the problems of life and art.

"I have a friend in Tel Aviv," he mused, "who is a very sensitive man.

"He didn't like the nose of the Russian ambassador to Israel. So, for that esthetic reason, one day he put a bomb in his garden."

The ex-Israeli surveyed the old gray brick building which now hides the library's beautiful architecture to the 6th St. side.

"That is an ugly building," he said.

"Perhaps I could call upon my friend's sensitive nature, get him over here, and ...

"Purely in the name of art, of course."

J. Chuter Ede, an absorbing Englishman, member of Parliament and former Atlee cabinet member, watched a "football match" on Channel 3 last weekend from his

Barringer Hotel room.

He didn't understand the game—but what really threw him were the commercials.

"An engaging fellow came on the screen," he recalled, "wearing the most somber expression.

"He said, 'More cars ... More horsepower ... More accidents.'

"What I expected next, of course, was a lecture advising everyone to respect the rights of his neighbor.

"But what happened?

"The fellow pointed his finger straight at me and told me to buy—

"More insurance!"

We are a sleepy Southern town no more.

Nobody even noticed Monday afternoon when a city bus stopped to pick up a Negro nurse with a Chinese tot in tow.

They had been waiting beside a Greek cafe owner in front of Trade Street's Tabriz Rug Co.

The Genial One

November 29, 1956

I WAS A STAMMERER FOR 27 YEARS."

It sounds like a speech course testimonial, but it's only the personal declaration of Genial Gene, he of the radio couplets and the glib tongue.

"Yep," he says, "I stammered worse than anybody you ever heard for 27 years. I used to evade speaking in public, and I'll tell you how I did something about it. I forced myself. I was teaching in the county and I was too poor to buy any literature for the youngsters, so I wrote little poems and plays. The English language has so many synonymous words that when I couldn't say one I'd just switch to another one. I had to learn words that way. I learned an awful lot of words, just so I'd have one ready when I hit one I couldn't say. That's the way I became a literary man."

His public, which tunes in WGIV at 6 and 11 a.m. and 1, 2 and 3 p.m. Monday through Saturday and all day on Sunday, gets an earful of literature.

Genial Gene (whose last name is Potts, by the way) talks in rhyme.

"I just make it up as I go along," he says. "After learning all those words to quit stammering, rhymes are easy. Sometimes it's hard NOT to talk in rhymes."

Genial Gene won top disk jockey laurels in the city a couple of years ago, after 1,000 votes from Central High School pushed him over the top. This week, he's celebrating his eighth year on the air.

"I belong to the public," Genial Gene explains. "I've m.c.'d at all the swanky clubs around here and things like that. But I try to stay on the giving end, keeping others happy."

On the "giving end," he's on the TB Association board, works with the March of Dimes, the Boy Scouts, the YMCA, United Appeal, Elks, AME Zion Church, and more civic committees than you can wave a microphone at.

"I don't have sense enough to say no." Genial Gene finishes work on his "Christmas committee" and sprays that Yule geniality over the air.

It goes like that all the time.

A press release from New York the other day described the Carolinas Carrousel as "a big holiday celebration known as 'Genial Gene Day.' "

The press agent was a little over-enthusiastic.

But give the ol' stammerer a few more years.

Workman, Spare That Stair

November 30, 1956

THE CASUAL, EVERYDAY, COMMONPLACE SCENe at right is soon to be banished from memory. For they are going to build a new YMCA off the beaten path on Morehead.

As sure as they do, the old YMCA on South Tryon will be demolished. It is not a lovely building and in this vale of progress someone will pick the site for an office building honeycombed with steel and glass.

We have no sympathy for that modern structure to-be, because it won't have steps.

The YMCA steps are the only steps worth mentioning in the whole course of Tryon St.

They are bold and shameless steps of granite. In themselves, they are things of utility and worthy of note, but our special plea is for the people they accommodate.

The YMCA steps were good enough, after all, for our fathers. For half a century, they have been something for after-school swimmers ("tadpoles," "speckled trout" and "sharks" or whatever those divisions are) to race up big-eyed and walk down later with wet hair.

They have supported the firm tread of businessmen heading for the steam room, the Atlas stride of weight lifters, the lithe bounce of handball players.

The special deity which protects the cherished monuments and institutions of man needs to be invoked in this hour.

No more YMCA steps? What, then, will beckon the stranger who stands on a windswept corner looking down cold streets for a sign, a token?

What, then, will serve to break the monotonous modernity of storefronts and skyscrapers?

And most important of all, where will a man sit?

The places to sit are being obliterated from this town. There is, to be sure, the Jack Bomar bench on Church St., but it is small. There are the DAR benches in the cemetery back of First Presbyterian Church, but some do not choose to rest themselves in a cemetery, particularly at night.

The YMCA steps are an invitation to sit, to read a letter from home, to digest the day's news or the evening's meal. For all we know, the YMCA plans to have steps on Morehead St., but it will hardly be the same.

There is nothing that can be done about it, we suppose.

But in the name of parade watchers and transients, "sharks" and handball players, pugilists and body builders—a sizable constituency—we would simple like to issue a demurrer to the demolition of hammers to come.

December 1956

He was very much a man of seasons. If it snowed, snow had meaning to him; if it was raining, rain had meaning to him. He had great sensitivity toward things—that was very clear in the beginning.

—Julian Scheer,
reporter, *Charlotte News*

Saturday Night Queen

December 3, 1956

THE CITY IS A WOMAN. Who wishes to deny it?

To her Saturday night subjects waiting for a bus on the Square, she is icy Queen Charlotte wearing a tiara of Christmas lights.

To a truck driver passing misty cafe windows on Trade St., she is a big-shaped, broadminded babe wearing a gaudy dress.

But whoever or where, she is all woman on Saturday night.

Down on Pine St., she is an old woman, tired and gone to bed right after dark.

At Memorial Hospital, around by the ambulance entrance, she is wide awake, quiet but sleepless, a nervous, dangerous lady.

On the broad avenues to the south, she is all charm and prosperity, perfectly composed, a genteel mother.

In a dozen drive-in lots, she is an Elvis Presley fan drinking a chocolate milkshake, craning her teenaged neck to spot her friends and giggling at boys scratching off in their fathers' cars.

She's a take-it-easy woman on Saturday night, and she has plenty of friends.

They nestle in her protecting arms if very young or very old. They drink to her at the country club or leave a bottle of beer to give her a juke box tune.

On McDowell, she's laughing; on the boulevard, she's humming; on a hundred nameless streets, she's sleeping, or weeping, or watching the boys go by.

In sum, she's a gay gal, and a good one.

Who she is—depends on who you are.

The Fabulous Jump-Up

December 4, 1956

IT IS TIME FOR A PERORATION ON JUMP-UP NAMES. They can be found in the funny papers and in Damon Runyon stories, of course, but in Charlotte they exist in the day-to-day conversation of our citizens. They are our own little scrap of folklore. The anthropologists of the future will remark on them.

If you followed our recent Great Shoeshining Contest—won by "Horsefly" Simpson over "Scoop" Antley by a whiskbroom hair—you are familiar with the phenomenon. Only people don't say "Horsefly." They say Horsefly. Just like Joe or Bill or other such wan, colorless names.

So there are people walking on Trade and Tryon known as "Bad Eye" or "Popcorn" or "Snake." That is not the way mothers would have had it, but that's the way it is.

The local expert on jump-up names is Donald MacDonald (not a jump-up name, by the way, but the Christian handle of an ex-police reporter.)

"Jump-up," he explains, is the name which suddenly jumps up at the sight of a person. Once it has jumped, it is likely to stay for life.

The court annals are loaded.

There is the case of "Sweet Pea" Stover, who was found by 12 good men and true to have shot a female friend on a North Charlotte corner.

There is "Pig Meat" Alexander, who has wept his way to immortality before the bar of justice in pleading his own drunkenness cases.

There is "Paregoric Annie," so named for her affinity to anything in a bottle.

People named Rhodes from Texas are bound to be named "Dusty." Even so, people with red hair are, *ipso facto*, "Red." Charlotte jump-ups are more imaginative.

There is "Red Light" Smith, a timid thief who pulled a respectable burglary some years back, but was caught when he stopped for a red light in making his getaway.

Among the ladies, there is "Stormy Weather," who used to make the water choppy for the Recorder's Court judges and cause them to wish they had forsaken jurisprudence in their youth.

There is a regular hierarchy of jump-up names in this town. "Lawyer" Helms must defer to "Governor" Broughton, the popular newspaper vendor of S. Tryon St.

Similarly, the "Duke of Salisbury," now passed on, a colorful gent with a passion for attending midtown weddings, ranked beneath "Queen Esther" when she was in her prime.

It is a glorious gallery, withal. Name your infant "Debnam" if you wish.

There, there, little Debnam, don't you cry. You'll be "Hang-Ear" by and by.

Frosty The Smokeman

December 5, 1956

AMONG THE VAST ARMY OF CITIZENS in this town with whom not even a six-armed newspaper reporter would exchange jobs is Charles S. Frost.

Up before dawn to sniff the atmosphere, he then rushes to the roof of City Hall to train field glasses and camera on Charlotte's chimneys. After that, he frowns over complex machines that inhale soot and record its density. After that, he calls up tough-minded building owners to preach them the gospel of cleanliness. After that, he writes letters, clips newspapers, speaks to civic clubs, prays for rain, writes reports and studies date. Then it's time to run on to the City Hall roof again.

Charles S. Frost is a rare bird. He is a smoke engineer. Those grim, dank, dark mornings—like yesterday—hurt him more than they do you.

You might think all Charles S. Frost has to do is talk a few janitors into being careful about smoke and pretty soon, he'd be out of a job. That's all you know.

"You want me to tell you what pollutes the air, eh? Charles S. Frost takes a deep breath. "All right—

"Smoke.

"Little bits of tires that wear off on the streets.

"Exhaust fumes.

"Dirt from cars that come in from the country.

"The natural erosion of buildings.

"Debris from trucks.

"Unpaved lots.

"Buildings being torn down.

"Stores sweeping dirt into gutters.

"Fumes from gas tanks.

"Cotton lint."

At this point, his eyes roll wildly.

"And you know what the firemen (not the kind that fight fires, but the kind that start them) say to me? They say, 'Well, the smoke has to go somewhere.'

"What I'm trying to tell them is that if they build a fire properly in proper furnaces, there won't be enough smoke to speak of—and they'll save money.

"This is something you can't tell some people.

"Rugged individualists. Bah."

What Charles S. Frost doesn't like is inversion. Inversion is when cold air acts as a lid to hot air in the city and won't let the smoke rise.

"But," he says, "you can't get rid of all particles in the atmosphere. If you did, as a matter of fact, the sun would be so hot, it would burn us all up."

A small comfort, however, when you can't see the Liberty Life building from the City Hall roof.

The Young At Heart

December 6, 1956

T HE STUDENTS WERE SUPPOSED TO BE the great friends of Russia," Steve said.

A look of wry amusement, of rather grim humor came to the eyes of this refugee of three weeks.

"That was the great surprise the Russians had in Hungary. The students crossed them up."

The students were always crossing somebody up, in Hungary and everywhere else. Unlike the plodding burgher or the established professional man, the student is unpredictable.

The Russians found that out in Budapest. It was the students who fashioned Molotov cocktails out of wine bottles. And it was the students who first poured into the streets to throw them at Russian tanks.

And now, here was Steve, telling the story to a silent and thoughtful audience of Davidson College students.

They understood. They were students. There is something in the soul of a student that abhors restrictions. This feeling about the value of freedom will take the form of a panty-raid, if there is nothing else handy to revolt against.

If there is a dictatorial government about, however, the dictator better duck.

Students are a restless and a reckless breed. A few years after they graduate into the market place, they grow in stodginess. As they lose their hair, they may also lose their stomach for a fight.

But while they are students, they managed to combine courage and common sense to an uncommon degree. And every once in a while, the older generation is shocked by some of the brutally frank and forthright declaration from the campus—or, as in the case of Hungary, some foolhardy and admirable action.

"If they'd leave it to the students, the kids would work it out okay," a college president told CBS' Eric Severeid once.

He was speaking of the segregation problem, but his suggestion is equally valid for a lot of the other thorns in mankind's side.

Unfortunately, governments have neither the will nor the desire to leave it to the students.

If they did, you felt while watching the Hungarian named Steve speak to his counterparts at Davidson College, the kids would, indeed, work it out okay.

Steve spoke to his audience through an interpreter.

But they talked the same language. It was the language of the student, a hopeful and meaningful tongue.

Trench-Coat Tales

December 7, 1956

W HEREIN WE TURN UP TRENCH-COAT COLLAR, don dark glass-es, and offer tells of intrigue, tell yarns of mystery and high adventure and reveal the Story Behind The Story:

A tough-looking hood stood in front of the Federal Reserve branch Wednesday afternoon—casing the joint.

"That's where they have all the money," he said. "There's a guard in there, but I bet I could run past him fast and get all the money and get away."

He was dressed in a bizarre cowboy suit and held a Halloween mask, classic disguise of all the Brinks robbers.

He surveyed the job coldly but he didn't get a chance to pull it off.

Because his mommy finished parking the car, took his five-year-old hand in hers, and walked away with him.

There is in this town a Jekyll-Hyde personality living a dual life. To reveal his name would be to end it all, so we will leave it shrouded in darkness.

But This Much Can Be Told:

By day, he is a senior at North Mecklenburg High School.

By night, he is a Charlotte College sophomore.

By the time he graduates from high school, you will note, he'll be halfway through college.

It happened in Gastonia:

Lady called the cops.

"My kitten," she said. "My Siamese kitten. It is missing. It has lovely blue eyes and the softest, silkiest fur you've ever seen ... "

An impossible task. But the cops said okay lady, we'll look for the kitten.

The word went out to the squad cars—

"Lovely blue eyes, soft, silky fur—"

Just as the search was beginning, a bedraggled tomcat walked out of the shadows. Nobody knew where he came from.

He set the kitten gently on her porch and disappeared into the darkness.

By The Dawn's Early Light

December 10, 1956

THE NEW DAY COMMENCES AT MIDNIGHT, but dawn is the real beginning.

Dawn is when the sleepers rouse themselves behind a hundred thousand drawn-blind windows, feel the narcotic of night ebb away and feel the reality of daylight creep into their bones.

Dawn is when the neon lights blink off, one by one, suddenly. They yield to the mottled pink that sweeps half the horizon, that silhouettes the buildings on Tryon St., that reflects in a silver sheen from the pavement where the water truck has just gone by.

Some people see dawn.

The policeman on the Square see it, from the first pale whitewash in the sky. He watches impatiently as the cars that hum past go—first one and then another—to parking lights, then no lights at all.

A janitor hosing out garbage cans behind a Trade St. hotel sees it. The dawn mixes with the high spray of cold water that the air catches and wafts down the alley.

An old man shuffles out of a 4th St. rooming house and

sees it. He stands for a minute on the sidewalk, buttoning his coat and looking toward a quarter of the sky where it is a dirty dawn, all soot and all too familiar.

The night is charitable. It covers a thousand imperfections of architecture, public health and private humanity on every block. The dawn is too revealing. It shines straight into the blood-shot face of every wino who dares look at it. It caricatures the ugly buildings. It causes a pile of rags in a Mint St. gutter to cast a long shadow.

The Trade St. groceryman puts the key in his lock at dawn, and when he opens the door to turn on the lights, the accumulated warmth hits him in the face.

Next door at the all-night cafe, the white fluorescence still outshines the sun. In an hour, the sun will take charge. But at early dawn, the glaring whiteness still commands a square of the Trade St. pavement.

Dawn is when the stainless tip of the Gothic steeple of old First Presbyterian glitters bravely.

Dawn is when a cab driver pulls into a loading zone, stashes his clip board over the visor and lets a cup of coffee out of a thermos bottle steam him awake.

Dawn is when a man wearing a tie looks out of place and gets "What are you doing here?" look from the tieless ones whose tieless occupations have brought them out at this hour.

Dawn is subtlety growing obvious. When the white square from the cafe lights is paled by the sun, the traffic will be heavier, the Negro maids will cluster at the Square awaiting those buses marked "QUEENS ROAD" or "EASTOVER," the street lights will go off, it will be over.

People start moving at 8 a.m., but dawn is the real beginning.

Coffee Break

December 11, 1956

EVERY EYE OPEN, that's our motto. An alert mind in a caf-feine-soaked body. Bring back a nickel cup of coffee.

Hither and yon, as was pointed out in this newspaper recently, the phenomenon survives, a benevolent dinosaur in an age of spacemen.

We are not talking about the nickel cup of coffee that goes with the meal. Nor do we recognize the free fill-up that follows the roast beef. Even the *gratis* coffee of DAR luncheons and airline flights is out, for purposes of this discussion.

We are talking about when you walk in to a commercial eatery, plunk down a nickel, say "Coffee, please," and get it. That is a nickel cup of coffee.

It exists. It exists at two midtown Colonial Store snack bars. It also exists, we are now informed, at Stanley's Super Drug out on E. 7th St. and at George's Grill on N. Caswell Rd.

Salud! May the circle widen. And what we'd really like to hear about is a restaurant owner who sat down by himself in some quiet place, meditated on his 10-cent coffee in terms of universal peace and good will, the universal design to steam one's insides on a frosty morn and the universal delight of a bargain-happy public, and decided, by crackle, to reverse the trend of the six-cent soft drink, the seven-cent ice cream and the eight-cent cigar by saying—

"What this jernt needs is a good five-cent cup of coffee."

We spent part of an afternoon with some non-coffee drinkers, the only "People" who really matter at this time of year, the starry-eyed small fry in the toy departments.

Hanging over Santa's shoulders and listening is like peering into the soul of youth.

"I'm tired of oranges in my sock," one little boy said. "Could you put a watch?"

Another took a deep breath and said:

"My little sister is scared of you so could you bring her nice presents and if you had time come to her room and kiss her?"

Talking to Santa Claus is a tight-fisted, lump-in-the-throat experience for most youngsters. They approach him with a mixture of eagerness and hesitancy.

"I've been a bad boy," Jimmy Lingerfelt of Concord said, "but if you'd go ahead and bring me ... "

He stop, then blurted out:

" ... the bike, I'd be good all the time."

It is a fortunate man who lives to have an experience as full of joy and mystery as this one.

Lady Launcelot

December 12, 1956

T HE FIRST COMMANDMENT FOR PUBLIC OFFICIALS in this town henceforth shall be borrowed with revision from Ladies Home Journal:

"Never Underestimate The Power Of A Woman Named Mrs. C.A. Jolley."

There are a few who made that mistake back in September. They have lived to rue the day.

Mrs. C.A. Jolley is the diminutive, innocent little housewife who got stoplights for Cotswold school children.

The stoplights, a High Commission announcement said yesterday, are going up right away. Three months ago, they were saying such a thing was "out of the question." That was before they got to know Mrs. C.A. Jolley.

All she can talk about now are the people who "did it." Well, she's the one who did it. Here's how:

"I went to see the highway department. They said it was just impossible.

"So I went to see the state sign man who writes SCHOOL on the highway. He came out, and looked it over. He said there just couldn't be a stoplight.

"So I went to see Chief Whitley. He promised to help all he could. I made a flag and stood out there with the Marines from the Reserve Center and the policeman and flagged the cars down.

"Then we got up a petition and went to the County Commission. Mrs. Ike Lowe helped. Mrs. Lowe wrote it and I typed it. Then Mr. Hardison came down and my neighbors all went up there and filled the Commission room twice.

"Then I went to see Ben Douglas. Then I wrote Mr. Hardison several times. I called him up. Then Sandy Graham in Raleigh said the stop signs—we got the stop signs—would have to come down.

"I lost 10 pounds and the doctor said, 'Those stop signs are where your 10 pounds went.' Everybody left the boat. People jabbed at me. I jabbed right back.

"I was going to see Luther. I told Mrs. Lowe we had to go see the governor and she was going with me.

"Somebody kept pulling the stop sign down and the police kept putting it back up again.

"I called everybody I could think of. People started coming out there again and looking. I went to the County Commission meetings and the commissioners said they'd go to Raleigh. They did.

"I had to stop smoking. And then the commissioners came back and they told me, 'We got what we went for.'

"You know, the people really came through.

"My children found something in a book about Davy Crocket where he said one time, 'Know you're right, then go ahead.' "

Mrs. C.A. Jolley is satisfied that she was right.

And next time a sweet young housewife comes walking in and smiles at them, there are those around here who will take their feet off their desks.

This time they got hotfoot.

Christmas Carol

December 13, 1956

C HRISTMAS IS COMING. Here's how you tell:

A girl stands on tiptoe to peer over a department store counter, grips the counter top with one hand and two dollar bills with the other, while a clerk wraps a bottle of perfume.

Fruit cakes replace angel food in the bakery windows; toys establish a beachhead in the Ivey's rug department; Perry Como and "White Christmas" take the place of Elvis Presley and "Love Me Tender" on dime store loudspeakers; Christmas trees, including pink ones, crown vacant lots; watches, a dollar down, a dollar a week and all set at 8:20, fill jewelry store displays; and on the Square, the dinner bell rings for charity.

A letter arrives from Bill Hodges, Charlotte trumpet man, touring the Orient with the Benny Goodman band. His itinerary: Now 'til the 22nd, Bangkok; the 24th, Singapore; the 25th, Kuala Lampur, Malay ...

What Christmas is like in Kuala Lampur, we cannot say. Presumably the strangers there turn their thoughts to home, wherever it is. And this side of Malay, people sit at their desks planning quick trips back to Statesville, to Spartanburg, to Hornersville, Mo.

A cart passes down W. 4th St., pulled by a husky, smiling man, loaded with pasteboard boxes, bearing on the rickety back of a holly wreath.

The calendars arrive in the mail, with pictures of Grandfather Mountain, etchings of the Saints, drawings of pretty girls.

Also in the mail is a piece of gentle defiance of Gen. Maxwell Taylor, who suggested Christmas cards clog up the system at the Pentagon and attempted to ban them this year. "Spread the joy of Christmas," our correspondent wrote, "Send a greeting to Gen. Maxwell Taylor, Pentagon, Washington 12, D.C."

The lights are strung. The collection cans are in place in every elevator. The trees, including the pink ones, are selling. The Post Office is becoming crowded.

Some may conclude it is a strange way to celebrate this birthday. The test is the human test, how you feel about it. The cart puller, the gift buyer, the charity collector—they feel good.

The Ping-Pong Ball's Secret

December 14, 1956

Physics and charity meet at the little pond in the S&W Cafeteria.

Since 1932, when the building was constructed, people have been idly eyeing that amazing ping-pong ball, the one that perches incongruously atop a squirt of water. They also toss pennies into the wishing well.

Nobody ever designated it a wishing well, understand, or invited anybody to contribute to it. There is apparently something in the human psyche that requires them to throw coins into a pool.

"We clean it out every now and then and contribute money to some current worthy cause," Jimmy Sherrill explains.

The haul is sometimes sizable. Once, so help us, we saw a water-soaked dollar bill lying on the bottom.

But back to that ping-pong ball. It just sits there, with, as they say in the Domestic Court hearings, no visible means of support.

"It has been there for 24 years," Mr. Sherrill says. "We have to change ping-pong balls occasionally, but they last an amazingly long time.

"The secret is to prick it with a pin and put a little water in it. That weights it down so that it settles into the center of the stream of water coming up from beneath it.

"A lot of people think there's a string under it and run their finger through the water to see. There isn't, of course."

That ping-pong ball is the principal attraction of mid-town Charlotte and to certain youngsters we know.

Day before yesterday, Don Hovis finished his lunch early and rushed to the edge of the shallow little pool to examine the phenomenon. Upon discovering the coins, naturally, nothing would do but that he hold up Mama for every penny in her purse and deposit them, one by one, at the bottom.

But after the pennies had settled to their places, Don got back to that ping-pong ball. He watched it bobbing and turning with the look of a tomcat about to show a mockingbird who's boss.

"When it falls," he said to the grown-up standing next to him, "I'm gonna get it."

But of course it didn't fall. When his mother led him through the swinging doors, he was still looking back, waiting.

That it doesn't fall is a fact full of mystery for even those small-fry who accept airplanes, automobiles and Superman with a sophisticated shrug.

And some of Don's pint-sized peers have not been so patient. This is one of the vicissitudes of the wishing well business.

"Every now and then," Mr. Sherrill remembers sadly, "I see a youngster reaching for the ball. Then—splash!"

The pool is not deep enough to be dangerous. And it is a matter of considerable pride around the S&W that they can fish out any young seeker after the secret of the ping-pong ball in five seconds flat.

Nobody Knows Who

December 17, 1956

N O PHOTOGRAPH CAN ACCOMPANY THIS ONE. For this is one about a man whose name and face nobody know.

Only his deeds are known. In a hundred houses racked with hardship and illness, his deeds will bring a prayer of thanks this month. To the people inside them, this nameless, faceless man is the spirit of Christmas.

It happens this way every year.

Each two-man team of Mecklenburg County patrolmen receives an order to pick a family, or two, or half a dozen, which is faced with extreme poverty at Christmas.

It is not a hard job for men whose daily occupation takes them all year into secluded corners of both the rural county and the human heart.

They talk to the parents. They may also talk to the Welfare Dept. They go shopping. On Christmas Eve or Christmas morning, County Police squad cars fan into the county on errands quite different from the ones they ordinarily perform.

"Once you've been on one of those things, you never forget it," a patrolman says. "Once you see the looks in the eyes of those little kids ... "

"Or their parents," another one remembers. "They always want to know where it all comes from. Last year, I bought food and toys and everything."

"That's the way he wants it," they'll tell you. "If they need shoes, get 'em shoes. If they need coal, buy coal. If they need the house rent paid, pay it."

When the job is done, the patrolmen give the bills to the desk sergeant. They tell him how many families they visited, how many people were in each family. He gives them their money back.

The benefactor, whoever he is, gets the bills for a Christmas present. He never sees the look in the eyes of the kids. He never even finds out who the families are.

The first shopping has already begun. Patrolmen Meredith Craig and Lindsey Burden went out this weekend to buy food and furniture and Christmas presents for a family who lost all those things in a fire last week.

By the 25th of the month, life will begin to ebb back for the family.

The bill will go to the desk sergeant, and somebody will pick it up.

Nobody knows who, and nobody asks.

The New Army

December 19, 1956

P ULL UP A CHAIR, Sarge, and leave us tell you about the New Army.

Robert Muhl, Ed Scott and Dick Pridgen just got back, see. They signed up in June and they're home in time for Christmas.

That's the way it works nowadays, for boys between the ages of 17 and 18-and-a-half. They got a special six-month tour for 'em, Sarge, and since you remember the day when nobody thought the Army was a good deal, we just wish you'd listen:

"It's really great," Bob said.

"The time passes fast," Ed said.

"I sorta hated to leave," Dick said.

You'd a been touched, Sarge.

Now the boys are home, in time for Christmas, and planning to go to college, find jobs and attend meetings of the 108th Division Headquarters once a week out at the Army Reserve Center.

"The food was nothing but the best," Bob said.

"We had the best company on the post," Ed said.

"The officers were terrific," Dick said.

Things, as you can see, have progressed, Sarge.

The boys got their training at Fort Jackson, S.C., just a hundred miles from home. After they finished their basic training, they came home every weekend.

Some of the stories they told as they sat and talked with the 108th's hometown commander, Maj. Gen. T.M. Mayfield, would have sounded familiar to you, Sarge.

"Shots on top of shots," Bob said.

"Chugging up that hill with 46 pounds on my back ... " Ed said.

"Those three days at the personnel center ... " Dick said.

The soldiering trio is out rounding up more converts to the special six-month program now.

"Just a big old family," Bob says.

"Everybody's the same age," Ed days.

"It's great," Dick says.

The proof is in the product, Sarge.

Ed lost 45 pounds.

Dick and Bob gained 15 each.

The Back Seat Cedar

December 20, 1956

YOU CAN'T DO ANYTHING TO CHRISTMAS.

Starve it and it becomes more precious. Inflame it with pain and it heals the pain. Hang it with gaudy ornaments and its real meaning shines like a diamond pendant in a box of beads, brighter by contrast.

Despair and distance couldn't do anything to the Christmas of Mrs. James Starke.

She and her husband were canvassers for the people who put out city directories in America's municipalities. Together, they traveled the states of North Carolina and Tennessee.

And since the city directory comes out early in the new year, Christmas was always a busy time of knocking on doors and inquiring about names and ages and telephone numbers.

Still, Mr. and Mrs. James Starke always managed to get home for Christmas Day. When their children came, Christmas became the best time of year—the one day when everybody was together in the little house in Kingsport, Tenn.

This Christmas will be the same. Except James Starke won't be there. He died this year.

And Mrs. Starke, hurrying along the streets of Charlotte, knocking on doors, questioning people within the houses, won't be able to reach Kingsport until Christmas Day. As always, this is her busy season.

Mrs. James Starke, working from a rented room, had no place for a Christmas tree.

Until she got her idea.

And that is why you may see a car with Tennessee license plates on the streets of Charlotte during this season with a Christmas tree in the back seat.

It has glass bulbs and tinfoil icicles and a star on top.

You can't do anything to Christmas.

10-4 For Christmas

December 21, 1956

Y ES, VIRGINIA, YES, YES, YES:

Christmas comes even to the place where teleprinters clatter, the police radio squawks and the coffee drinkers on the copy desk start their day at 6 a.m.

Preachers, politicians, press agents, publicity men, paupers and poets send Christmas cards. The Christmas card is the greatest democratizer since the Model-T Ford and the .45 pistol. The pauper's is more valuable than the prelate's.

Odd little stories come through the newsroom doors in this season. Unimportant things, when viewed in the context of "important" things going on in the world.

It is a matter of record, for example, that a well-dressed man walked up to the Salvation Army worker at the airport and handed him a $10 bill.

Through childhood, he said, he had wanted a red wagon. He never got it. Could the Salvation Army, please, buy a red wagon for some boy?

An inconsequential thing to almost everyone in a month when $10 bills pass at such speed from hand to hand.

But Maj. W.H. Arnold says the man's eyes were clouded

when he walked away. They will contrast with the bright eyes of a boy looking at his first red wagon Tuesday morning.

Christmas comes silently and swiftly. Elizabeth Blair Prince writes about the legion of empty stockings that hang hopefully four days before Christmas. Helen Parks writes about churches and their various interpretations of the meaning of it all. Emery Wister writes about Christmas wreaths and lights and trees. Julian Scheer writes about a man who will do anything for $250, literally anything. Bud Cox writes about the endless shelf of "Treasures" that gremlin presses roll out each December. Society writes about Society, of which the nature of the holiday dictates, there is much. Photographers take photographs of kids and angels and Santa Claus with real beards.

The coffee machine in the hall which sits there saying nothing all year suddenly says something: "Merry Christmas." And the "coffee man" gets a name, Paul Leopard Jr.

The calm voice of the police radio assures the big room that peace on earth, good will to men is a reality. "Ten-four," it says. That translates, "Okay. All is well."

They have hung a sprig of mistletoe in the sports department. It may not be just Christmas that is coming, but the Millennium.

Silent Night

December 24, 1956

S ILENT NIGHT, HOLY NIGHT ...

The blind man shuffled down Tryon St. singing the carol softly, almost under his breath. It was anything but a silent day. People talked and laughed as they passed him. Horns honked in his ears, a bus pulled away from the curb and drowned a phrase of his song.

All is calm, all is bright ...

All was nervous, loud, doubtful and dark. He moved his feet cautiously. His faced screwed into a troubled protest to the clamor of the street. He strained to hear the clank of coins that dropped occasionally into his cup so he could acknowledge them with a nod. Sometimes he even failed at that. In the midst of the din, he went on with the carol.

Round yon Virgin, Mother and Child ...

Round the blind minstrel, the shoppers swirled. A teen-ager laden with packages bumped his shoulder and squealed, "Oh, EXCUSE me!" He missed a chord and swallowed a phrase:

Holy Infant, so tender and mild ...

The tune was tender and mild, but the going was tough. The sounds around him were harsh and brittle in the crisp December air. The song seemed out of place and the singer caught in a cold tide.

Sleep in Heavenly peace ...

The song went on, but nobody listened. There were things to buy and people to see and places to go in a hurry. The singer sang on, a bit louder, but his words were lost in the loud preparation for the silent night. The night was coming, but in the afternoon, the rushing forms he couldn't see swept past him and the only soft and quiet thing on Tryon St. was his voice.

Letter to Scrooge

December 25, 1956

D EAR EBENEZER,

Marley is dead. And so, of course, are you.

Not in the trite sense that you will "live forever," but in the ordinary, daily, simple meaning of the word. As a practical man, which you always were, you will understand this.

The proposition we have to offer you today concerns your descendants. There are Scrooges, Ebenezer, with us yet. Oh, they are good people at heart, just as you were. But just as you were, they are misinformed about Christmas. Do you suppose you could clank your chains at 'em?

First there are those who grumble about how much "trouble" Christmas is. Of course, it is. Always has been, from the first one, which was so much trouble for that couple from Nazareth that they gave up looking for a room and settled for a stable.

Fighting the crowds on Tryon St. is no fun. The Bethlehem crowds are the same. And earlier Christians than we had to fight the Roman soldiers to celebrate Christmas. We miss the meaning of it all to commemorate the "trouble."

Then there are lesser Scrooges who decry the "commercialization" of Christmas. They mean people are knocking themselves out to sell something at this season, and to that extent, they are right.

But did you ever run into a man who thought his OWN Christmas was too commercial? Doubtful, Ebenezer. One's own Christmas is all plum pie and spirituality. It is the other man who misses the true meaning of the day.

Perhaps you could help convince these frowners that Christmas does not abide in a shop window but in the human heart, an organ notably difficult to commercialize.

You may find it hard to take after your own awakening, but on this afternoon, Ebenezer, when the stab of excitement in the soul of childhood is giving way to the warm and sleepy afterglow—on this afternoon, on all afternoons, there are still people who complain about Santa Claus.

You would think the goodness of Santa Claus, who is a Saint, after all, had been amply demonstrated by now.

But they say the old guy has nothing to do with Christmas and should be banished. We have heard them say it.

Visit them, Ebenezer. Show them the compatibility of Christ and his birthday's Saint. Touch them with joy. Give them a testimonial. Soothe their fears about the future of this day. As even you found out in the end, it is the greatest day of all.

Wish them a Merry Christmas, Ebenezer. And the same to you.

The Dearest Dear Departs

December 26, 1956

T HE NATURE MUSEUM DEER IS LEAVING. Ten years of love have done him in.

To the young patrons of the museum, there is something unspeakably sad about this. Most of them do not remember the day in January, 1947, when the deer arrived from the Museum of Natural History in New York.

It was a proud dear then, newly gone from its woodland haunts, newly mounted, clear of eye and strong of limb.

It's a good enough deer yet to the younger undiscerning ones, but the truth is its ears are tattered from a thousand fond touches of a thousand children, its neck is split from hugging, its back is bare from being stroked by small hands.

In this season, the deer gets a red nose and becomes Rudolph, the fabled puller of the Christmas sleigh.

The sleigh will be unhitched when the week is over and the threadbare old deer will trot into Valhalla.

A replacement is coming, the museum folks hope, from the Hornaday Foundation of New York.

It will be a fine animal, undoubtedly.

But for the children, the ones who made the change necessary, he will never take the place of the worn and crippled deer making its last stand at the Nature Museum this week.

Hope For A Weary Week

December 27, 1956

T HIS IS A DEADLY WEEK FOR US CALENDAR WATCHERS. There may be a raggier week somewhere, but we have shuffled through the *Esquire* girl and we cannot find it.

Nineteen-fifty-six is so crotchety and old it is not worth living with, and brisk little 1957, the brat, is not yet here.

This is the week of faded tinsel, broken candles, and stale eggnog.

The travelers at the airport last night fell into this mood. A sailor sat with his chin in his hands while his buddy slept, his white hat tilted over his eyes.

A pretty blonde girl leaned her pony-tail against the cool plastic chair she sat in and stared at the Christmas tree.

The Christmas tree was wilted. Its top drooped.

Half a dozen weary salesmen who knew perfectly well that nobody would be buying in this waning week stood in the concourse's cold, ready to board their planes and do or die for the corporation, and probably die.

A college boy held his girl friend's hand.

"Christmas was wonderful," she said.

But Christmas was over.

Or that's what we thought until the sign on the newspaper box hove into view. It had been put there by a *Charlotte News* carrier to whom the calendar meant less than the bulge in his change purse.

Where the sign beside the coin slot ("5c daily, 10c Saturday") had been, there was a large piece of cardboard, lettered in red:

"Anything you give me. Take one. Free If You Feel That Way. Thanks."

And under it, as an afterthought:

"We want you to be happy."

There is hope for world, of course, even in the tattered remnants of such a tail-end week as this.

Exercise In Imagination

December 28, 1956

T HIS WILL NOT BE EASY, but try:

Try to imagine a foreign flag whipping in the wind over City Hall.

Picture, if you can, a dictator's photograph in the window of the drug store in your neighborhood, and a dictator's informant behind the counter.

The stores on Tryon St. still are there, but a new suit costs more than you can earn in two months. An automobile is beyond your wildest hopes.

Now try to imagine rebelling in your mind against the state of affairs, going to your closet where you have hidden a rifle, taking it out and loading it.

You walk down your driveway and into the street, where your neighbors are milling about. Together, you walk into town.

At the police station, you and your neighbors find fighting. People are crouched behind trees on the Courthouse lawn, shooting across the street to the windows. Men at the windows are shooting back.

You go on up Trade St. toward the Square. There, a building is on fire. Machine guns rattle. A block away, a bomb explodes and shatters the shop windows.

At the Trade St. underpass, you meet a tank, its heavy gun leveled at you, its tread chewing up the street. The tank fires, a cornice crumbles, and your best friend who had been walking beside you, falls dead on the sidewalk.

The whole city is full of fumes and chaotic sound. Men rush into stores and throw books and papers and pictures out into the street, and set fire to them.

No place is safe. Snipers on the College St. rooftops clear the street. Whenever you see a man now, he is running.

Out in the suburbs, children are lost from their parents, squads of soldiers patrol the shopping centers. Everywhere, there is smoke ...

When the smoke passes, you can see Charlotte. Not that way, but as it is.

That is the way Eva and Geza of Budapest, Hungary, saw it this week, with the December sun slanting down on the calm trees and cool lawns, with people filling the midtown sidewalks.

Perhaps you could not imagine it any other way.

They can.

That is why Eva and Geza, who have been here two days now, like Charlotte so much.

He was unpretentious, eager, interested in people, interested in people on the staff, interested in the city. Everybody liked him. He was very easy to get along with, and it didn't take very long for everybody to sort of conclude that here is a guy who is going to go places.

—Julian Scheer,
reporter, *Charlotte News*

Kuralt Of News Wins Pyle Award

January 15, 1957

CHARLES KURALT, 23-year-old *Charlotte News* reporter, has been named a 1956 winner of the Scripps-Howard Ernie Pyle Memorial Award.

Mr. Kuralt and Gordon S. (Bish) Thompson of the *Evansville, (Ind.) Press* each received cash awards of $1,000 and bronze medallion plaques which annually go to the two newspapermen whose writing and reporting is judged as "most nearly exemplifying the style and craftstmanship" of the great World War II reporter and human interest columnist.

Mr. Kuralt, who joined the *News* staff in May, 1955, scored with a collection of feature stories that appeared in *The News* in a column called "People." They included such off beat subjects as a one-armed banjoist philosopher, a Rescue Mission poet, a little girl's sunny afternoon frolic in an ancient cemetery, and a mountain lad's impressions of his first visit to the city.

"Kuralt's writing," the judges commented, "is sensitive, warm with affection for obscure people, and with excellent touches of humor where that is needed." ...